Praise for
NORTH KOREA CONFIDENTIAL

"James Pearson and Daniel Tudor have shown that we don't have to rely on intelligence leaks and disinformation in trying to fathom North Korea. There is solid information out there, which they have brought together and augmented with solid personal insights and first-hand reporting, worked into a readable and informative guide to real life in the DPRK. It's a useful addition to a small number of good modern works on North Korea."
—Martin Uden, former British ambassador to South Korea

"Pearson and Tudor have expertly distilled a deep study of North Korea into a comprehensive yet highly readable account of the economic, informational and social forces that make North Korea go round today. From the differences in fashion trends in Pyongyang and Chongjin to the co-operation of regime officials and private market traders, *North Korea Confidential* is stacked with insight and details. For anyone seeking to understand North Korea beyond the headlines of the Kims and missiles, this book is a must-read."
—Hannah Song, CEO of Liberty in North Korea (LiNK),
an NGO working with North Korean defectors

"Tudor and Pearson's timely book goes a long way to counter the lazy stereotypes that provide the staple of global commentary on North Korea. This beautifully-written account of daily life shows that North Koreans of every age routinely bypass government restrictions as they participate on a day-to-day basis in self-interested market-driven activities. Young North Koreans watch South Korean movies, listen to K-Pop, copy South Korean fashions and like young people everywhere, find ways to meet up with partners outside the restrictions of parental supervision. The authors do not minimize the authoritarian nature of the North Korean state but they make a hugely important contribution in taking seriously the difference between government policy and the reality of daily life. This book is a must read."
—Hazel Smith, author of *Hungry for Peace: International Security,*
Humanitarian Assistance, and Social Change in North Korea

"The book isn't just invaluable for expanding our view of North Korea beyond the cliche, soda-straw view of Pyongyang and showing us the gritty, anarchic country in which most North Koreans live, or at least survive. By explaining how thoroughly capitalism has already penetrated North Korea, it should cause experts to question the long-held assumption that 'communist' North Korea is destined to be reformed by capitalism. Indeed, *North Korea Confidential* shows us a North Korea that has settled into a new set of contradictions—already capitalist, yet as repressive and militarized as ever, a command economy bifurcated between the Inner Party and everyone else, where the rich are getting richer and the poor aren't."
   —Joshua Stanton, human rights campaigner, blogger and media critic

"This book is a fascinating insight into the DPRK by two leading British journalists. Pearson's and Tudor's extensive research draws on a range of sources to analyse aspects of North Korean society that are so often hidden from view. A compelling read for anyone with an interest in real life in the DPRK."
   —Scott Wightman, British Ambassador to South Korea

"Books on North Korea continue to flow off the press. Some are polemics, some are alarmist, but this work by two journalists looks at real life. In fluent and measured terms, it depicts how the majority of North Koreans really live. Its focus is on those who wheel and deal outside the official system who have become the new elite in the North. Their new wealth may be precarious and small by the standards of their neighbors but it is real and it is transforming the North. Well worth reading."
   —James Hoare, former Charges des affaire at the British Embassy in Pyongyang

DANIEL TUDOR & JAMES PEARSON

NORTH KOREA CONFIDENTIAL

Private Markets, Fashion Trends, Prison Camps, Dissenters and Defectors

TUTTLE Publishing

Tokyo | Rutland, Vermont | Singapore

Published by Tuttle Publishing, an imprint of
Periplus Editions (HK) Ltd.

www.tuttlepublishing.com

Library of Congress CIP data in progress

ISBN 978-0-8048-4458-1

Distributed by:

North America, Latin America & Europe
Tuttle Publishing
364 Innovation Drive, North Clarendon
VT 05759-9436, USA
Tel: 1 (802) 773 8930; Fax: 1 (802) 773 6993
info@tuttlepublishing.com
www.tuttlepublishing.com

Japan
Tuttle Publishing
Yaekari Building 3rd Floor
5-4-12 Osaki Shinagawa-ku
Tokyo 1410032, Japan
Tel: (81) 3 5437 0171; Fax: (81) 3 5437 0755
sales@tuttle.co.jp;   www.tuttle.co.jp

Asia Pacific
Berkeley Books Pte Ltd
61 Tai Seng Avenue #02-12, Singapore 534167
Tel: (65) 6280 1330; Fax: (65) 6280 6290
inquiries@periplus.com.sg; www.periplus.com

18 17 16 15   5 4 3 2   1506CM
Printed in China

The Tuttle Story
"Books to Span the East and West"

Many people are surprised to learn that the world's leading publisher of books on Asia had humble beginnings in the tiny American state of Vermont. The company's founder, Charles E. Tuttle, belonged to a New England family steeped in publishing.

Immediately after WWII, Tuttle served in Tokyo under General Douglas MacArthur and was tasked with reviving the Japanese publishing industry. He later founded the Charles E. Tuttle Publishing Company, which thrives today as one of the world's leading independent publishers.

Though a westerner, Tuttle was hugely instrumental in bringing a knowledge of Japan and Asia to a world hungry for information about the East. By the time of his death in 1993, Tuttle had published over 6,000 books on Asian culture, history and art—a legacy honored by the Japanese emperor with the "Order of the Sacred Treasure," the highest tribute Japan can bestow upon a non-Japanese.

With a backlist of 1,500 titles, Tuttle Publishing is more active today than at any time in its past—still inspired by Charles Tuttle's core mission to publish fine books to span the East and West and provide a greater understanding of each.

Contents

Introduction

*D*id you know that the average North Korean lives off the proceeds of capitalism? Or that at least half of all North Koreans have seen South Korean TV dramas and movies, and listened to South Korean pop music? And did you know that North Korean soldiers spend more time working on private construction projects than on plotting the destruction of Seoul?

These days, "Pyongyangology" has become a cottage industry, inspiring the creation of a huge number of books, newspaper articles, and documentaries. Unfortunately, there are few accounts of how North Korea really works today, with regard to both the Pyongyang elite and the average citizen. It has become natural when dealing with North Korea to focus entirely on Kim Jong Un, geopolitics, or the regime's nuclear weapons program—but to do so is to miss the huge amount of internal change taking place, both at the top and bottom of North Korean society.

It may surprise the reader to learn that North Korea is now quite a dynamic place. The average North Korean breadwinner makes a living from private trade; people have official jobs in state-owned factories, but are able to bribe their way out and conduct business of their own. Women close to the Chinese border wear skinny jeans, in spite of their illegality. Most young adults in Pyongyang possess cell phones, and when they seek out romantic liaisons, they have the option of renting someone's home for an hour or two.

Rich and poor alike do, indeed, enjoy listening to South Korean pop music, in utter contravention of the government's wishes. And as throughout the rest of Asia, North Koreans are becoming addicted to South Korean TV shows, obtained from China on DVDs, USB sticks and micro SD cards. In most cases, anyone arrested for possessing South Korean media will simply end up paying a bribe and walking free. This is because North Korea has become an extremely corrupt society over the past two decades or so. In fact, the most money-hungry North Koreans are to be found among the elite—those whom one might have assumed to be the most ideologically "pure" members of society.

The typical account of North Korea is written with admirable sympathy for the nation's long-suffering citizens. Such accounts, though, tend to strip those very same people of agency, reducing them to dehumanized caricatures—the brainwashed Kim Il Sung worshipper, or the helpless victim of the state security apparatus, for instance. The latter certainly does exist, and thus, we do present a chapter on what constitutes crime and punishment in North Korea. However, it is important to remember that the average North Korean's chief concerns are more ordinary: just like people anywhere else, North Koreans are concerned with making money, raising their children well, and occasionally having a little fun. Increasingly, North Koreans are able to satisfy these needs beyond the umbrella of the state.

The main cause of North Korea's recent social change is actually a tragic one: the famine of the mid 1990s, in which at least several hundred thousand people perished. The famine greatly weakened the bond between the state and the people, forcing the average North Korean to fend for him or herself. As a result, the government is now just one part of a quasi-capitalist market economy, rather than the sole coordinator of economic activity that it once was. Time and again throughout this book, the reader will notice the influence of the famine as an agent of social and economic change.

Throughout Korean history, there have been examples of calamitous events leading to huge social upheavals, and eventually, unexpected progress. From the ashes of the Korean War (1950–53), for instance, rose a generation of meritocratic and extremely determined nation-builders in South Korea. The authors believe that North Korea's greatest tragedy, the famine, will one day be seen as a similar spur to progress.

One Caveat

Reporting on North Korea presents a huge journalistic challenge. There is a lack of reliable statistics about the country. The opportunity to canvass "the man on the street" in Pyongyang on his opinion of Kim Jong Un—and getting an honest answer—comes up very rarely (though the probability is greatly increased when one shares a bottle of *soju* with a North Korean living abroad). However, we have done our best to present as accurate a portrait as we can, by talking to experts who we trust (some well-known, others less so), and to sources drawn from different sections of North Korean society. Such sources include elite members of Pyongyang society still very much on the "inside"; defectors of different ages, geographical origin, and year of departure; diplomats and NGO workers; and, traders and other border-crossers places like Yanji, a Chinese town forty minutes drive from the North Korean border. We also make use of text sources in English, Korean, and Chinese. As a general rule, we decided to consider reliable claims made by three or more separate and credible sources. The reader may, of course, have different criteria.

We do not, therefore, offer this book as the last word on North Korea, and so we politely ask the reader not to have such expectations. After all, one would not take as the last word a short book claiming to tell you the whole story of today's USA, either. Our hope is that you will consider *North Korea Confidential* an informative introduction to the real story of modern North Korea—that of not just the leadership, but also the dramatically changing lives of 24 million people who live there.

Thanks and Acknowledgments

Many wonderful people were kind enough to share their time and insight with us during the writing of this book. Unfortunately, some of them would get into trouble if we thanked them for that here. But those who we can thank publicly are, in no particular order:

Michael Madden, Shirley Lee, Sokeel Park, Jang Jin-sung, Andrei Lankov, Chris Green, Matthew Reichel, Curtis Melvin, Simon Cockerell, Andray Abrahamian, Monique Macias,

Those who we have not thanked above, you know who you are, thank you.

Also the authors wish to thank the following friends, co-workers, and relatives who provided support or tolerated canceled appointments and the like, or who are just nice people to whom we wish to express our appreciation.

Daniel's thanks: Mum and Dad (and all my family), Kang Kyung-nam, Kang Se-ree, Ku Min-jeong, Kim Bo-yeon, Yoo Je-hoon, Ku Young-shik, Chun Su-jin, Kim Jong-hyuk, Lee Seung-yoon, Jung Young-sun, The LFG family, Kim Nam-hoon, Lee Yoon-hee, Yoon Sun-oo, Kim Yong-moon, Han Sang-hyuk, Lee Ji-eun, Sung Ki-wan, Song Jeong-hwa, Moon Jung-hee, Park Soo-jin, 'The Korean', Tom Coyner, Lee Jae-woong, Lee Seong-hee, Sohn Mi-na, Song Ji-na, Bobby McGill, Yang Sung-hoo, Kim Hee-yoon, staff and patrons of The Booth (our fine craft beer establishment!), David Maltby,

Kwon Yong-ho, Andrew Barbour, David Chance, Naomi Rovnick, Tyler Cowen, Michael Freeman, Ryan Anderton, Geoffrey Cain, Jung Yoon-sun, Park Jae-uk, Lee Seul, Lee Yoo-jin, Lee You-kyung, Chris Backe, Kang Jeong-im, Ji Bae and family, Zachi Schor, Guy Biran, Cho Young-sang, Andrew Salmon, Cho Sung-moon, Pyo Chul-min, Heo Eun-sun, David Pilling, Lin Lin, Krys Lee, Kieran Ridge, Hannah Bae, Darren Long, Chico Harlan, Bill Miller, Antti Hellgren, Robert Koehler, Ambassador Vishnu Prakash, Dennis Vartan,

James' thanks: Mum, Dad, and the extended Pearson-Mantle family and friends; Hyojin Kim; Doris Carding; David Chance, and the Reuters Seoul Bureau, especially colleagues Tony Munroe, Jack Kim and Ju-min Park, and Darren Schuettler and Sebastian Tong in Singapore; the Department of East Asian Studies at Cambridge especially John Swenson-Wright, Mike Shin, and Barack Kushner; Korea and China folk at SOAS especially Jim Hoare, Michel Hockx, Xuan Li, Jaehee Cho, Jae Hoon Yeon and Kyung Eun Lee; all at the British Association of Korean Studies, and the British Korean Veterans Association; the Korea Foundation in Seoul; at NK News Chad O'Carroll and Gianlucca Spezza; a special mention to Simon Cockerell, Curtis Melvin, Sokeel Park, Michael Madden, and old friends near and far of whom there are far too many to mention.

The following English language sources were invaluable to us. The keen reader may note that they collectively represent a wide range of the ideological spectrum on North Korea analysis, but all individually possess very strong merits, and thus we recommend them for anyone seeking to know more about how North Korea works:

Books & Publications

Collins, Robert. *Marked for Life: Songbun* (2012)

Cumings, Bruce. *Korea's Place in the Sun* (2005)

Haggard, Stephan & Noland, Marcus. *Famine in North Korea* (2009)

Jang, Jin-sung. *Dear Leader* (2014)

Kang, Hyok. *This is Paradise!* (2007)

Kretchun, Nat & Jane Kim. "A Quiet Opening: North Koreans in a Changing Media Environment," InterMedia (2012)

Lankov, Andrei. *North of the DMZ* (2007)

Martin, Bradley K. *Under the Loving Care of the Fatherly Leader* (2004)

McEachern, Patrick. *Inside the Red Box: North Korea's Post-totalitarian Politics* (2011)

Myers, B.R. *The Cleanest Race* (2011)

Websites

38 North website (38north.org)

Daily NK website (dailynk.com)

New Focus International website (newfocusintl.com)

NK Economy Watch (nkeconwatch.com)

NK Leadership Watch blog (nkleadershipwatch.wordpress.com)

NK News website (nknews.org)

North Korea Tech (northkoreatech.org)

Rimjin-gang/ASIAPRESS (asiapress.org/rimjingang/English)

Sino-NK (sino-nk.com)

Both authors also tweet about North Korea:

Daniel Tudor @danielrtudor

James Pearson @pearswick

A note on the romanization of Korean

North and South Korea differ on the romanization of Korean. Where possible, the authors have used North Korean convention in the romanization of North Korean names, places or concepts. South Korean convention is used for South Korean names and places, and for expressing spoken sentences in Korean. So Kim Jong Un (not Kim Jeong-eun) lives in Pyongyang (not Pyeongyang).

Chapter 1

The North Korean Markets: How They Work, Where They Are, and How Much Things Cost

"Communist," and "collectivized" are utterly outdated labels for a North Korean economy that now heavily relies on thriving, person-to-person market exchanges in which individuals buy and sell private property for the purpose of generating profit. Private trade has become so prevalent in recent years that it permeates all levels of society, from the poorest through to the Party and military elites. But as with sex in Victorian Britain, there is a double standard with capitalism in the Democratic People's Republic of Korea (DPRK): while everybody does it, few publicly admit to its existence.

Though markets in some form have always existed in the DPRK, the declining official role of the state in economic activity means that private trade has never been as widespread—or necessary—as it is today. The reason for this is simple: the state can no longer provide for the people in the way it once could.

As we shall see, the horrific famine of the mid-1990s was

the turning point. Regular, government-supplied food rations all but disappeared during this period, and never fully returned. The lesson that survivors took from this experience was one of self-reliance—not the self-reliance of *Juche* ideology, but rather self-reliance through by-hook-or-by-crook capitalism. Private property and private trade remain illegal, but for post-famine North Korea, there is but one real economic rule: don't follow the rules. Sixty-two percent of defectors surveyed in 2010 stated that they had engaged in work other than their official jobs before leaving North Korea, and a thriving gray market that uses unofficial currency exchange rates is now the de facto way of setting prices, even for the elite.

The Breakdown of the System

From the foundation of the DPRK in the 1940s, North Korea was almost food self-sufficient for many years. Under the Public Distribution System (PDS), farmers turned over a majority of their harvest to the government, which then redistributed it to the wider population. During the earlier and middle years of Kim Il Sung's rule North Koreans were not wealthy, but they at least did not starve en masse. Older Chinese living near the DPRK border have been known to remark that they envied the living standards of North Koreans in the 1960s and 1970s.

The North Korean economy, in fact, performed quite well throughout the late 1950s, 1960s, and early 1970s. The North's command economy was stronger than the South's state-capitalist model on a GDP per capita basis until around 1973. This was partly due to historical circumstance: due to its proximity to Manchuria and China, the colonizing Japanese (1910–1945) had elected to industrialize the northern part of Korea, whilst using the south as an agrarian "breadbasket." Thus, the North had a head start over the South in the form of superior infra-structure. This, combined with a general fervor to rebuild a battered and divided nation, helped drive the North Korean economy in those early years.

There was one other crucial factor in that initial success: Soviet and Chinese aid. Throughout the Cold War era, North Korea was able to exploit the rift between China and the Soviet Union by cleverly playing the two against each other. In this "love triangle" relationship, North Korea would carefully seek benefits from both Beijing and Moscow, turning its weakness as a "shrimp between whales" into an asset. This strategy, which is echoed in the regime's continued ability to exploit the concerns of China and the United States to its advantage, resulted in a steady flow of aid, helping bolster the people's food rations. North Koreans, though, were not told that foreign aid put food on their table: the government allowed them to believe that it all came from the munificence of Kim Il Sung.[1]

Against the expectations of many, the DPRK managed to survive the collapse of the USSR in 1991. This was partly due to increased Chinese aid, and the fact that the people still generally trusted in the regime.[2] However, the decline and then total cessation of Soviet help—plus growing economic mismanagement under Kim Jong Il—began to put the PDS in

---

1. It is, however, quite common to see rural North Koreans using sacks marked "US AID." It is unlikely they know what this means, but the sacks have the Korean for "A gift from the American people" stamped on the outside.

2. Government control of information flow will also have aided the regime in the short term. To illustrate, the Tiananmen Square massacre became known to some Pyongyangites simply via word of mouth, but most North Koreans would never have heard about it at the time. By contrast, they were most certainly allowed to hear about the 1980 Gwangju massacre in South Korea.

jeopardy. Gradual decreases in the amount of food distributed were instituted, with 10 percent reductions in 1987 and 1992, for instance. But it was not until the early to mid-1990s that the system began to completely break down.

The economic situation was already extremely fragile, and North Korea was already entering a food deficit by 1993. Things were ultimately exacerbated by a series of devastating floods in 1994 and 1995, which destroyed around 1.5 million tons of grain and ruined much of the nation's infrastructure. Around 85 percent of North Korea's power generation capacity was lost as a result. The PDS came under unprecedented pressure: between 1994 and 1997, the basic ration was cut from 450 grams of food per day to a meager 128 grams. In the same period, the PDS went from being the main food source for a majority of the people, to a resource that only six percent of the population could receive.

The result was a serious famine between 1994 and 1998 that claimed the lives of between 200,000 and three million North Koreans.[3] The state refers to this calamity as the "Arduous March," the name of a legendary wartime campaign said to have been waged by Kim Il Sung as a young guerrilla fighter. It may be seen as darkly ironic that the North Korean state's greatest failure—and the one that effectively ended the socialist economic system that Kim Il Sung "marched" to build—has been dressed up in such terms.

Starvation gripped society on a horrific scale. Inland, rural areas were worst affected, but mass deaths from famine happened in every part of the country, including in towns and cit-

---

3. There is much debate over the final human cost of the famine. Official UN population figures show no significant decline in the population during that period. None of this, however, should be allowed to overshadow the overwhelming tragedy of the 1994–98 period itself.

ies. The government had failed the people, and crucially, everyone had to fend for themselves. Even professors at Pyongyang's prestigious universities had to turn to low-level market activities, simply to survive.[4] Some would join their wives outside busy train stations or colleges, selling cheap broth made from flour and water. Other members of Pyongyang's lesser elite circles took to selling their household possessions at knockdown prices in makeshift market stalls.

Thus, the famine sowed the seeds of marketization in North Korea. Only the core elite can now live on food handouts.[5] Just like the university professors who became street hawkers to survive, the majority of today's North Koreans have learned to lead an economic double life in order to make ends meet. Though born out of tragic necessity, this is a development that is today having a significant impact on the lives of ordinary people, making their situation more tolerable.

Crucially, the famine also empowered North Korean women to aspire to be more than just homemakers, many becoming the real breadwinners of the North Korean family unit. It is mostly women who run market stalls, sell food, engage in small-scale import–export, or rent out the family home by the hour to courting couples. All this, in turn, is having a dramatic impact on the role of women in society, and even on the rate of divorce. Traditionally, the north of Korea was considered more "macho" than the south,[6] and even after the arrival of Com-

---

4. One member of an elite Pyongyang family states that her family had enough to eat during the famine, due to government handouts. Her friends in the same apartment building though were not; her family shared their food with them

5. Though they, too, now participate heavily in market activities, as they are the ones best placed to benefit.

6. Even the way North Korean men talk is more manly; they apparently consider the way South Korean men speak to be effeminate.

munism—which is theoretically supposed to pursue gender equality—a North Korean woman was typically seen as some man's daughter, wife, or mother. Today, she may have independent power. In the past it was rare for women to use *banmal*, the informal level of Korean speech, toward men, although men would often use it when speaking to women; this convention is now weakening.

Won (and Yuan) for the Money

The DPRK government has a complex and difficult relationship with this new economic order. The eradication of capitalism in North Korea would greatly increase the possibility of another famine, given the failure of the command economy and the PDS. Furthermore, many government insiders are now using trade as a means of generating personal wealth, as we shall see later in this chapter. If full market reform were pursued though, it would result in huge social and economic changes that could threaten the government's position. There are, indeed, reform-minded public officials in North Korea, but there is also a natural fear of change at the top. For a member of the elite, full economic liberalization may eventually lead to exchanging a privileged existence for prison, death, or more prosaically, the life of a taxi driver in Seoul.[7]

Keen, then, not to go down either the controlled Chinese or chaotic East European routes of abandoning political ide-

---

7. The former President of Sierra Leone, Valentine Strasser, may be considered luckier than some deposed dictators, in that he lives as a free man in his own country. However, he makes do on a US$50 per month pension, and lives in a slum with his mother. He reportedly drinks gin all day long to forget about his dramatic fall from grace.

ology in favor of economic reform, the government has gone to great lengths to control the rise of private market activity. There are occasional crackdowns on marketplaces, for instance. And in 2009 came the bluntest move of all. That November, it was announced that the national currency, the North Korean won, would be redenominated via the cancellation of the last two zeroes on every banknote. A 1,000 won note needed to be exchanged for a new 10 won note, and so on. Citizens were given one week to trade in their old zero-heavy notes for new ones. Similarly, a bank deposit of 100,000 won became 1,000 won at a stroke.

Though one may speculate over the government's motives, the measure essentially functioned as a cash grab, destroying the wealth of private traders. Why? Because each person was only allowed to convert a maximum of 100,000 won (around US$30–40 at the time, according to black market rates). Anyone holding a sum greater than that—as someone engaged in business naturally would—saw their savings wiped out.

The outcome appears to have been anger directed against officials of a severity not seen in North Korea for a long time. Though the 100,000 won limit was raised to 150,000 won in cash and 300,000 won in bank deposits, it appears that this did not halt public discontent: the Chinese Xinhua news agency reported "collective panic" among North Koreans, and other media reports claimed that piles of old notes were being burned in protest against the redenomination. If true, the latter would be particularly telling, as the destruction of 100, 1,000, and 5,000 won notes necessarily involves the destruction of images of Kim Il Sung.

The anger of ordinary traders would no doubt have been compounded by the fact that the real elite of North Korea tend to hold their assets in other currencies, particularly the Chinese yuan.[8] Even prior to the redenomination, the North Korean won was not a currency in which people placed much trust, and so those with the opportunity—such as officials conducting quasi-public, quasi-private business with Chinese counterparts—kept their earnings in foreign currency.

But again, the long-term result has been to push North Koreans even further beyond the orbit of state economic control. Ordinary people now increasingly seek out the yuan and other currencies as stores of wealth. They have learned not to trust the government and its currency, the won. At the same time, they have learned that trading and saving in yuan can shield them from the consequences of future government depredations and incompetence. As a result, a majority of market transactions in North Korea are now estimated to be conducted in foreign currencies, with the yuan being the most favored.[9]

It is hardly surprising, then, that the unofficial, gray market value of the North Korean has been sinking. Though there is an official government-set exchange rate of 96 won per

---

8. If you visit North Korea, you will also be expected to use Chinese yuan or euros. Before the early 2000s, foreign visitors were able to use won— or rather, a separate won unavailable to Koreans, in order to keep the two camps separate. Cuba does this still with the peso and the chavito. Unlike Cuba, however, North Korea offered two kinds of won: glorious red banknotes for those from friendly socialist countries, and suspicious blue ones for capitalist running-dogs and imperialist lackeys. Today, however, even foreign tourists can get their hands on North Korean won by changing money at gray market rates in a select few banks, department stores, or sometimes on the street. But like the exchange rates on offer, doing so is a legal gray area, and some tourists may be duped by a skilful seller into handing over a fist of Yuan in return for a few souvenir notes.

9. From c. 1997 until c. 2004, the dollar was the preferred foreign currency. When North Koreans feared U.S. sanctions might hit their dollar supplies, they theoretically switched to the Euro, which were in shorter supply. Now, however, the Yuan is taking over.

US$1, the "real" rate is around 8,000 at the time of writing—and that number has increased dramatically over recent years, with the declining trust in the Won. Tellingly, even North Korean banks are now moving much closer to the black market rate, often changing at rates that slightly undercut the black market prices. In the Special Economic Zone of Rason, Golden Triangle Bank was even exchanging US$1 for 7,636 won in mid-October 2013. There are also reports that workers at a handful of large, state-owned enterprises, such as Musan Iron Mine, had their wages increased from 3–4,000 won per month to 300,000 won per month in September 2013, to reflect the won's real value.

Black market pricing of the won is even becoming common in ordinary shops and restaurants. For example, a toy shop in Pyongyang prices basketballs at 46,000 won each; clearly nobody believes a humble basketball is really worth over US$400. Somewhat similarly, a department store selling such well-known Western products as Pepperidge's cookies, Hershey's chocolate, Ferrero Rocher, and Ceres grape juice, prices all of them at the official rate, but refuses to accept North Korean won.[10] The same is true of an entire Adidas store, stocked with sporting goods brought in from China (presumably without the knowledge of Adidas), at prices that would be extraordinarily generous if they could be bought in Won. The low won prices quoted are simply an indication that one must pay for these items in foreign currency, at a dollar price that reflects their real value.[11]

---

10. One could consider this a matter of saving face. No shopper is seriously going to ask why they cannot buy in won, as they already know the real answer.

11. In 2014 the government introduced a new 5000 won bill, the highest denomination note, that was not emblazoned with Kim Il Sung's face—

The dual valuation of the North Korean won does result in some interesting bargains, though. Public transport is still provided at a price reflecting the official rate, which means journeys are sold for much less than they are really worth. A trip on the Pyongyang Metro, for instance, costs five won. That is a mere five US cents even at the official exchange rate—and at the real rate, it is as good as free.[12]

Unfortunately, the same is true of salaries. All workers, officially at least, are employed by the state—and they are paid in accordance with the official value of the won. Civil servants, for instance, usually earn in the range of 1,000–6,000 won per month. At an official rate of 96 won per US dollar, that would already be bad enough—but when one considers the "real" gray market exchange rate, even a highly-ranked official is being paid less than US$1 per month.

Under a communist system of theoretically free healthcare, education, food, and housing, such a salary would not be as awful as it sounded. But as we know, the state can no longer effectively provide for the people (though admittedly, elites are still given some rations). Thus, the worker and his family must look for other ways of making money, usually in the market or by offering services of some kind. The result is that, in North Korea, everyone from the miner to the schoolteacher lives an economic double life of sorts, with many engaged in cash-in-hand jobs or market activity in their spare time to generate income.

---

thus indicating the late leader's visage will be saved for a new, higher denomination note of 10,000 or possibly even 50,000 won. Increasing the highest single-use note is yet another sign of the government recognizing (and accommodating for) the black market value of the won.

12. The day that the Pyongyang Metro starts charging 300 or 500 won instead of five could well be the day that the government finally signals acceptance of the market economy.

This phenomenon has extreme negative consequences for the ability of the country to function properly. Because people are paid virtually nothing, they have very little incentive to do much actual work. Police live for opportunities to extract bribes and many state employees will make extra cash by purloining workplace property, or using it for their own ends. A factory worker earns around 2,000 won per month, and thus it is no surprise that there are many reports of state-owned factories being stripped of anything made of metal, or of workers taking factory products and selling them privately. At the official exchange rate, a factory worker would not even be able to afford a pack of cigarettes with a month's salary, let alone the lighter with which to light them.

Inside the *Jangmadang*

Just as North Korea has two exchange rates, it effectively has two economies: the "official" economy (where people work in state jobs and are paid a state salary) and a "gray market" economy, where people earn money in ways that are not strictly legal, but widely tolerated. The latter is the one that really counts in today's North Korea.

The term used for the illegal, yet tolerated, markets in North Korea is *jangmadang*, an old-fashioned Korean word that literally translates as "marketplace" (South Koreans go to the *sijang*, a word also used in China) and has its roots in old-fashioned Korean farmers' markets. *Jangmadang* can often be seen at the busy intersections of narrow, muddy residential streets in rural North Korean towns or, on occasion, in specially-constructed buildings designed for market activity. Such buildings can even be seen on Google Earth; the clearest example of this was the blue roofed Chaeha-dong market, in the city of Sinuiju near the Chinese border. Unfortunately, the building was eventually pulled down, but this does not mean business in Sinuiju is over—trading has simply moved to other parts of town.

People setting up stalls in the *jangmadang* are required to pay a stall tax to Party cadres in order to keep their slots—thus making the state complicit in marketization. In some large markets, there are even electronic registration systems in effect, to keep track of who has paid their stall tax. And traders looking for new customers often transport their goods by hand over mountain paths, across rivers, and through muddy valleys or dusty tracks in order to avoid the prying eyes of government officials who may try to stop them or, more likely, demand a cut of the profits.

The typical *jangmadang* stall-holder is a lower or middle class *ajumma* (a middle-aged, married woman). Though Korean culture has been male-dominated since neo-Confucianism stamped its imprint on the Joseon dynasty (1392–1910)—with the ideal woman considered the one who lived as a *hyon-moyangcho* ("good wife, wise mother")—it was often the case among the peasant population that the women were the market traders, not the men. In South Korea today, poor old ladies sell vegetables and rice-cakes on street corners, and appear en masse outside metro stations with baskets full of umbrellas on rainy days. It is no surprise, then, that *jangmadang* traders in North Korea are usually female.

There is an additional reason that the *ajumma* dominates the *jangmadang*. In North Korea, adults are assigned to work units, to serve the state in return for pitiful salaries. Married women, however, are exempted from this. This means they are free to work as market traders. They can therefore earn significant multiples of what their husbands make, turning them into breadwinners and challenging the traditional Korean husband–wife dynamic.

There are, though, plenty of people with official jobs who engage in trading as well—it is not impossible for men to join women in trading, but rather, just a little more difficult. Sometimes, people disappear from their work unit for months, on the pretext of having to receive medical treatment; what they are really doing is trading in another part of the country. Everyone knows this, but nobody truly cares. The trader merely reports back to their local unit at the end of the period, and submits to a "self-criticism" session or pays a bribe before resuming their regular job.[13]

But what do *jangmadang* traders sell? As may be expected, there is a focus on the basics. North Korean cigarettes go fairly cheaply, but more sought-after Chinese and Russian cigarettes can cost anything from ₩2,000 (US$0.25) to ₩20,000 (US$2.50) depending on the brand. A bar of chocolate costs around ₩3,000 (US$0.38), and a kilogram of rice costs around ₩5,000 (US$0.63) Imperialist American Coca-Cola is very much available, and goes for ₩6,000 per can—about US$0.75, not far from what it would cost in a supermarket anywhere else. Cans of Chinese beer, such as Tsingtao or Harbin, cost ₩4,000 (US$0.50), pots of instant noodles are ₩7,000 (US$0.88), and a tin of instant coffee from China would set you back around ₩10,000 (US$1.25). But due to the extreme volatility of the North Korean won, all these prices may be wide of the mark by the time you read this book.

The image of the middle-aged lady peddling cigarettes and noodles from a little stall is hardly a sophisticated one. But the

---

13. These days, there is even an arrangement (the "August 3rd rule") whereby workers may pay a monthly fee of 50,000 won (around US$7) to be exempted from work, freeing them up to engage in private business. Effectively, then, this fee is a tax on private earnings.

economic nous of the wholesalers they buy from should not be underestimated. Rice traders, for instance, (illegally) monitor foreign radio in order to find out in advance about aid shipments into North Korea.[14] If a shipment is on its way, the market price of rice will fall due to the expectation of increased supply—and the race is then on to sell up before everyone else finds out. A big incoming supply of fertilizer will have a similar impact on the market, as it will have the effect of increasing rice production. Rice is as crucial to North Korean life as it always has been, and thus its price is the subject of great attention. The state still does not produce enough rice[15] and has to depend on aid or imports to make up the deficit.

Jangmadang trading is now commonplace all over the country. Even in Pyongyang, where state control and loyalty to the government are strongest, virtually every family will have members involved in such activity. The occasional tour guide—a person who undoubtedly has the trust of the regime—too will admit to foreign visitors that they have family members involved in *jangmadang* activity, or at least that they shop at them. Even if one is not selling goods, one may be involved in transporting them, sourcing them, or greasing the palms of officials to allow everything to continue. While one *ajumma* may be the public face of the business, her relatives and friends will likely be helping out behind the scenes. They may also have a "share" in the business: many *jangmadang* stalls are paid for by people clubbing together to raise the stall tax and buy the stock.

---

14. Much foreign aid to North Korea is corn, however, and rice is too expensive for many lower-class North Koreans.
15. Diplomatic sources running joint agricultural projects with the North Koreans and other foreign agencies say the food deficit gap is closing, although like any other crop, the weather can have a severe effect on the North Korean rice harvest..

It can even be dangerous to *not* be a trader. Middle- and high-income families that are not known to be actively engaged in business are at risk of being investigated by the authorities. Such a family would be assumed to have a less "tolerable" source of income, such as cash transfers from defector relatives living in South Korea. There have actually been many instances of people informing the authorities about neighbors who have money but no obvious business interests. This has led to the ironic situation of some North Koreans being observed *pretending* to be engaged in capitalism in order to avoid suspicion.

Following the Money Trail

But what of those less tolerable sources of income? There are around 24,000 North Korean defectors living in the South—equivalent to 0.1 percent of the North Korean population—and many more living in China. Though their lives are often hard and involve "starting again" at the bottom of the social and economic ladder, the money they can save even through basic, menial labor can actually make a significant difference to the lives of their relatives back in North Korea.

It is estimated that transfers to the North from defectors in the South amount to around US$10–15 million per year. This is not a huge sum overall, but if one considers it on a per-family basis, its potential impact should certainly not be overlooked. Typically, a defector who sends money home will transfer one million South Korean won (just under US$1000) per year; in a country as poor as North Korea, such an amount goes a long way.[16] Furthermore, according to a Database Cen-

---

16. For this reason, it is commonly said that an inspector with a defector-

ter for North Korean Human Rights survey in 2011, 12.5 percent of those who send money hand over more than five million South Korean won each year. Transfers have also certainly helped some people get started in the growing gray economy. Scarce wonder, then, that it is now seen as desirable to have defector relatives, where it was once deemed a disgrace—though any feelings of pride will not be expressed too openly.

There is no official system for the transfer of such funds into North Korea. Transferring money between South and North is illegal in the eyes of both countries (though the South is much more willing to turn a blind eye when the cash flows in a northward direction). However, there are well-established networks of agents who have devised quick and efficient ways of getting the job done—for a fee, of course. For the privilege of sending money to relatives in North Korea, a defector will expect to pay a commission of up to 30 percent. So for every million South Korean won sent, perhaps only 700,000 won will reach the intended recipient.

The size of the fee reflects the risks involved, and the relative scarcity of the service. Generally, the first step involves a defector finding a broker in South Korea, selected on the basis of personal recommendations from other members of the defector community. The sender will hand over money to the broker, who then wires it to an account in China. Another agent, possibly an ethnic Chinese living in North Korea (known as *hwagyo*),[17] checks that the money has arrived,

---

financed family in his area never need worry about his income. Of course, this is because he can extract bribes from them.

17. Ethnic Chinese in North Korea have much greater freedom to enter and exit the country. This privilege can be used to make money—arranging remittances, importing and exporting goods, and so on. For more information on *hwagyo*, please see chapter 7.

through mobile banking on his Chinese smartphone. Chinese mobile network signals can be picked up in border towns, so this can be accomplished without the agent having to leave North Korea. The money in the Chinese account is left untouched, and the agent simply picks up the equivalent cash from a stash of yuan already held in North Korea. If the recipient lives locally, the agent may pass on the cash himself;[18] if not, then another agent—this time an ethnic Korean—will be on hand to deliver it anywhere in the country.

One important feature of this system is the fact that agents also arrange phone calls between sender and recipient: the whole process is typically bookended by quick chats between family members. Agents are not just able to bring money into North Korea; they are also able to smuggle in Chinese cell phones, letters, and other items. Particularly in the case of North Koreans living near the border, it is a relatively simple matter to set up a short phone call to South Korea.[19]

Brokers are also quick. But again, North Koreans living near the border have an advantage here: there may even be a knock at their door within the hour of a relative in Seoul handing over a wad of cash. "It's quicker than Western Union," says one Seoul-based NGO worker who assists defectors. And they are more reliable than one might imagine. There are few reports of money going missing along the way, despite the necessarily illicit nature of the transfer process.

---

18. The cash is handed over in yuan—thus contributing to the "yuan-ization" of the northern regions of North Korea.
19. Since 2014, the North Korean authorities have been using more advanced techniques including cell phone signal detectors to root out illegal phone use. There has also been a fairly extensive crackdown on border-crosses on both the Chinese and North Korean sides.

An Economic Border

But isn't the border heavily guarded? How on earth does a Chinese smuggler cross into North Korea? Given North Korea's totalitarian image, it would be natural to ask such questions. But the Sino–DPRK border is actually very porous. While the Demilitarized Zone (DMZ)—fortified no-man's-land at the 38th Parallel between North and South Korea—is a "proper" border in the eyes of North Koreans, the northern border is more of an economic divide. At the DMZ, hundreds of miles of barbed wire, fences, and landmines keeps North and South Koreans out of mutual reach. But Sino–DPRK border crossings—both officially sanctioned and otherwise—are commonplace. In 2012, around 130,000 North Koreans visited China legally, using permits granted by the government. Such permits may take months to obtain through official channels, or be granted straight away if accompanied by a US$50–100 bribe.[20]

That is not to say that one may cross the border at will. The average North Korean would run a grave risk by attempting to just enter China without making arrangements first. Particularly since the latter days of the Kim Jong Il era and the early days of Kim Jong Un, border security has been much tighter, making defections difficult and more dangerous. But for those with connections and/or money, matters are relatively straightforward.

Chinese traders and North Koreans doing semi-private business in China may cross—though the latter are more likely to fly in from Beijing. Chinese traders make regular crossings

---

20. For the average North Korean, however, permission is unlikely to be granted. One needs a good background and connections. A well-connected broker could also get you out for a fee.

at border towns like Dandong, bringing with them all manner of items sought after by North Koreans. The South Korean "Cuckoo" brand of *bapsot* (rice cooker), for instance, takes pride of place in many high-income North Korean households. There is so much trade between North Korea and China that there are even goods made specifically for the North Korean market, such as televisions that run on very low power. And though the overall volume of trade is high, it is mostly conducted by small traders that authorities aiming to uphold UN goods sanctions would find it extremely difficult to monitor.[21]

It is also possible for ordinary North Koreans to bribe their way across the border. There is a well-established process whereby one family member makes it to South Korea, and starts sending money back home with the specific purpose of facilitating the defection of their relatives. Brokers with the right connections will, for a fee, physically take them across the border into China. In the "basic" defection package, the new defector will then be left to his own devices, most likely to make the long and perilous journey across China and into countries like Thailand or Mongolia via further illicit border crossings. But there are even "gold" packages (which may cost around US$10,000) that give the new defector an escort from their home all the way to Beijing, and the requisite false documentation to get them on a flight straight to Seoul.

Moreover, regional geography lends itself to simple border-jumping. For some stretches of the 320 mile (520 km) long Tu-

---

21. The average Air Koryo flight from Beijing to Pyongyang will also be loaded full of flat-screen TVs and other high-end items, purchased by North Korean traders in China. There are in fact shops near the DPRK embassy in Beijing aimed specifically at North Koreans, created for this purpose. Knowing this, one must again question the efficacy of sanctions enforcement.

men River that marks the most northeastern corners of the border, the gap between the two banks becomes so narrow that passersby on the Chinese side can see washing hanging from the lines of North Korean houses. Even at wider areas, the relatively shallow depth of the river, its tendency to freeze over during winter, and its various rocky spits and sandbanks make crossing the Tumen a fairly easy affair, border guards notwithstanding.

The source of the Tumen is Paektusan, the most revered mountain in Korean culture, and the mythical place of origin of the Korean people. It was there that Hwanung, the son of Hwanin (the Lord of Heaven), was said to have descended to earth to establish Sinsi, the "City of God." His own son Dangun later founded the first Korean kingdom, Gojoseon, at a city named Asadal near present-day Pyongyang. It is natural, then, that Kim Jong Il's official propaganda would (falsely) claim him to have been born at Paektusan. But while Paektusan is as critical to the Kim family myth as it is to Korea's creation myth, the river that flows from it is a source of opportunity for many North Koreans seeking a new life away from the DPRK.

Public-Private Partnerships

Much of the attention given to the "new capitalism" of North Korea centers on the ordinary people who are now able to make a living through *jangmadang* trading, small-scale import–export, and the selling of services (the fixing of bicycles, for instance). But bottom-up business in the DPRK is outstripped in size and scale by what might be cynically referred to as "public-private partnerships."

Since the mid-1990s, the North Korean government has been in a state of almost complete economic failure. It maintains strong political control of course, particularly in Pyongyang. But the central government cannot generate enough direct revenue or tax income to fund its myriad departments, ministries, commissions, and committees. Due to this lack of central funding, government organizations have, essentially, been left to their own devices. And though their provision of services to the people has decreased dramatically in recent years, they still need to function at a basic level. They also need to pay their staff—or rather, find ways for their staff, who receive pitiful official salaries (of a few dollars a month, at black market rates),[22] to get paid. The ad-hoc solution has been for officials to start quasi-private businesses under the umbrella of their organization. It is therefore no coincidence that the invitation lists of Kim Jong Il's famed drinking parties began to change in the 1990s. They used to simply contain the names of his most trusted officials, but his new favorites from that time on became those who could make money.

There is certainly no formalized system for how such businesses are started and operated, and no "typical" example. But a successful case might run as follows. A member of a government entity (such as the National Defense Commission, whose senior members "can do whatever they want," according to one source) with good political connections and permission to travel abroad will seek out joint ventures or import–export opportunities in China, or even further afield. Food, agricultural supplies, medicine, and consumer luxuries are considered particularly important areas. Once a plan is formed, an officially state-owned firm will begin to pursue the opportunity, as privately-owned companies are still considered illegal.

---

22. State salaries, although meager, still come with some tokens that can be exchanged for food. Therefore, although the money itself is useless, the small amount of rations it provides is a useful supplement.

Only some of the proceeds go to the state, though. Because North Korea has no proper banking system, firms tend to hold a lot of cash—and also keep financial records in old-style hand-written ledgers. A highly profitable firm can, therefore, very easily be turned into a modestly profitable one, allowing those who run the business to pocket around 60-70 percent of the earnings, with the rest going up the department, and higher-ups who need bribing. And because North Korea's economic system is not properly rule-governed, nobody is going to stop a protected insider from engaging in shady accounting. In this way, the organization can make a little money to help make up its budget, founders can become wealthy, and managers and executives (also typically employees of the same department) can respectively earn around US$300 and 500 per month in successful cases, according to one knowledgeable source. This is nowhere near what a manager in South Korea can make, but in North Korea, it can provide a very impressive standard of living.[23] Furthermore, talented managers will be able to lobby their bosses for permission to set up subsidiaries of their own; permission may take a year or two (and some bribery, of course), but the wait can be well worth it.

Just like revenues, production can also be underestimated. Agricultural produce, or goods made in a state-owned factory, can be made to "disappear" in this way, allowing the govern-

---

23. That said, the average South Korean company man works a little harder. In both countries, workers start early—it is custom to arrive at the office before your boss does. North Korean company men get in at around 7.30 am, and clean their office before having an 8 am meeting. Actual work starts at 9 am, with time at 12 noon for a packed lunch. In the afternoon, it is possible to have a nap until 2 pm—something that no self-respecting *chaebol* boss in Seoul would allow his workers to get away with. Following a 6 pm meeting, workers head home. Brow-beaten Seoul salarymen will still have a few hours to go at this point.

ment official/entrepreneur to make his profit. Invariably, these goods end up in the *jangmadang*. Though of a different socio-economic class to the average *jangmadang ajumma*, the elite trader will have ways of doing business with the former. Thus, about 20 percent of *jangmadang* product is estimated to be domestically produced (the rest being mostly from China).

Because all companies are officially owned by the state, the entrepreneur's security depends on his/her personal power and connections. There is a great deal of "horse-trading" over who gets to grab any lucrative opportunities. A would-be entrepreneur needs a sponsor—a very powerful person who will protect their position. Naturally, this also means paying kickbacks. In a sense, then, the top leadership of North Korea is operating a protection racket.

Those at the top also operate their own businesses. Prior to the power play that brought about his shock removal and execution in December 2013, Jang Song Thaek—Kim Jong Un's uncle by marriage and long-time Kim Jong Il-era power-broker—had famously wide-ranging business interests, and a net worth of around EUR 80 million, according to a very conservative estimate. Mr. Jang "owned" luxury hotels in China, for instance, and controlled much of the burgeoning Sino–DPRK border trade. His widow, Kim Kyong Hui, is understood to control the bottled mineral water company Kangso Yaksu, and the Haedanghwa corporation, which operates department stores and is involved in the DPRK's overseas restaurant businesses. Ms. Kim was also until recently the ultimate guardian of the Kim family wealth. These assets are kept in banks all over the world and may total US$20 billion, according to sources.

DPRK-owned Korean restaurants operate in many cities in Asia and Europe—there are over 40 in China alone, and a handful throughout South East Asia. Guests there are treated to musical performances of old Korean standards as they dine on *galbi* or *segyeopsal* (known in the South as *samgyeopsal*). These establishments are very popular with South Koreans, who find them both familiar and exotic. Sometimes, North Korean officials take advantage of this, planting spies among the waitresses, to build up profiles on visiting South Koreans who come to their attention for any reason. But the main reason they exist is to provide a slow trickle of hard currency for the regime and provide a front from which to mix legally earned cash with the proceeds of illicit activities.[24]

One well-placed source states that a typical North Korean overseas restaurant will be opened by a female relative of a senior official, such as a vice-minister. She will club together with a few friends to raise the start-up capital. This will be used to pay a kind of "franchise fee" in the low six figures (USD) to Kim family accounts, as well as the cost of actually opening the restaurant. The government will appoint staff, who are strictly monitored and who will also end up remitting most of their wages back to the center.

Additionally, 20–30 percent of profits must also be handed over on national holidays. It is apparently common for well-to-do North Koreans to be seen carrying large bags of cash through airports at such times of year. Not paying up would be very unwise, as it could cause severe trouble for relatives remaining in North Korea. The threat of the prison camp for loved ones keeps overseas North Koreans in line.

Some officials are better placed than others to make money.

---

24. According to reports by the United Nations panel that monitors the enforcement of UN sanctions on North Korea, a significant amount of hard currency also comes from illicit weapons deals with other states, including Syria, Iran, Libya, Tanzania, Somalia, Eritrea, Uganda, and Ethiopia, to name a few.

Those with the chance to gain foreign language skills and overseas experience have a great advantage, as they will possess the ability and contacts to conduct international business. It is thus common to hear of people bribing their way into diplomatic jobs, or into government bodies with real power.[25] Similarly, members of the Kim Il Sung Youth League, which participates in communist-related events around the world, can take advantage of their global connections to engage in profitable trade. The Youth League used to run summer camps for children from all over the communist world, prior to the fall of the Soviet Union; today, they run a trading corporation named Paekam, in addition to several restaurants and hotels in Pyongyang.

The Construction Industry

The army is heavily involved in construction, as a source of cheap labor for the building of apartment complexes, hotels, roads, bridges, and so on. Contrary to the popular image of the North Korean soldier as a goose-stepping, brainwashed loyalist and ruthless killing machine, the average military man is likely to spend more time building things than working to crush the "puppet" regime in Seoul. Even state media often refers to them as "soldier-builders."

Military units are now little more than free labor teams.[26]

---

25. Men with such jobs are also considered highly eligible, and will be able to marry into elite families to further cement their status. Since the late 1990s, Pyongyang has seen the rise of the financial-political power couple, who combine their respective advantages and pass them on to their children.

26. Their morale is also correspondingly low, according to many sources. The average North Korean soldier is exploited for his labor, poorly trained, and poorly fed. In the event of serious trouble, Kim Jong Un would probably not be able to rely on his rank-and-file troops, and

If the government needs a road built, the only major outlay will be on materials—the labor cost will simply be the amount of money it takes to feed the soldiers and, given that some soldier-builders are tasked with foraging for their own food, sometimes food costs nothing, too. And if a group of ambitious managers at a government ministry want to erect an apartment block, they can hire the army to build it, too. There is, in fact, a great deal of "soldier-built" public-private construction taking place in North Korea today.

As the construction of a big building is a much more complex (and expensive) task than, for instance, the importation of medicine from China, there are relatively few who can pull it off. But among those who can, there is apparently some degree of competition to get projects off the ground. There are two reasons for this. The first is, of course, the high profits that can result from exploiting dirt cheap labor. The second is prestige. A successful construction project can get an ambitious official-cum-entrepreneur noticed, leading to promotions and further opportunities, as long as everyone gets their cut. This is especially true in the Kim Jong Un era, where the state likes to emphasize economic development and prosperity in its propaganda.

Alongside public-private construction by various branches of the government, money from Japanese-Koreans also finances building projects. During the colonial era, many Koreans emigrated to Japan, and between 1959 and the late 1970s, around 90,000 of their descendants responded to North Korea's call to "return." This was done through an organization named Chongryon, which acted as a de facto DPRK embassy

would instead have to turn to a small number of combat-ready special forces soldiers. From an outside policy perspective, this further underlines the fact that the DPRK will never voluntarily give up its nuclear weapons, which remain its only real deterrent.

in Japan. Chongryon and its members continue to operate pachinko gambling businesses in Japan to provide funds for their newly-impoverished relatives, and the North Korean state in general.

Returning Japanese-Koreans were often treated with suspicion in North Korea, and lacked the connections necessary to live well in such a capriciously-run country. The one trump card they possessed was the ability to get money from relatives in Japan, who were comparatively very wealthy (and unlike defector-sent money, the DPRK government welcomes it). It became common for Japanese-Koreans to invest this money in construction. These days, Chongryon is in deep organizational decline, but there are still significant private capital flows into North Korea from Japan, and these have been put to use in building the Chongjin Hotel, for instance, and numerous apartment projects.

Some apartment complexes are built with specific tenants in mind—military veterans, star athletes, or scientists, for example. Ministry of Foreign Affairs apartments in Pyongyang are considered rather ritzy, as foreign ministry staff have grown used to such apparent luxuries as round-the-clock electricity on postings abroad, and expect nothing less when they return home. In a country where blackouts are very common and winters brutally cold, 24-hour electricity is a real indicator of who can be considered properly "elite," and who cannot.[27]

Just as in any capitalist country, apartments in North Korea can be traded. Probably a majority of units in an upmarket new-build apartment block will be sold on the market, rather than given to the state employees they were officially intended

---

27. If one has enough money, it is also possible to bribe one's way to an electricity hook-up from a nearby military installation or government office.

for. The only real difference is the lack of a formal system for apartment transfer, since owning private property is forbidden.[28] If you live in any North Korean city, however, it will be possible to "sell" your apartment: people living in the same district are legally allowed to swap homes, so this may even be done in a semi-legitimate fashion, facilitated by a cash payment,[29] though often, house trading is done without any registration at all. In Pyongyang, where apartment prices have risen more than ten-fold since the turn of the century, trading may even be facilitated by an (illegal) estate agent.

Apartments in ordinary areas and without lifts or reliable electricity[30] may change hands for as little as US$3–4,000. Lower floors command higher prices, though. It is generally accepted that the poorer you are, the higher up you live. This contrasts with South Korea, in which the best views are prized. But when there are no lifts—or a power outage can get you stuck in one—the top floor suddenly seems less appealing.

Homes near the Sino–North Korean border are apparently quite expensive, since living there offers good business opportunities, and the ability to access Chinese cell phone networks. There are reports of high-quality apartments changing hands for US$30,000 in the border city of Hyesan, for instance. But this pales in comparison to the upmarket areas of the capital:

---

28. Except in very rare cases, where a small, unmodernized house has remained in the possession of one family from before Kim Il Sung's land reform.
29. Sometimes, the officials processing the paperwork know exactly what is going on, and demand a cut for themselves.
30. Electricity supply is exceptionally weak in North Korea. Even the grandest buildings of Pyongyang, such as the People's Study Hall, must economize by either leaving their lights off, or keeping them on the lowest setting, for most of the day. They are turned up full when important guests arrive.

a decent apartment in the central Pyongyang district of Mansudae (which is now jokingly referred to by expats as "Dubai" or "Pyonghattan") will change hands for US$100,000 or more. There are even those who talk of US$250,000 apartments. That is a lot of money to spend on a place that you don't officially own. But if you have that kind of sum at your disposal in North Korea, you will be able to ensure that it stays yours.

Inequality

Those who visit Pyongyang regularly remark that the city is now undergoing a boom of sorts, and those with money are spending it openly. A few years ago, if you were wealthy, you kept it quiet and discreet—now, flaunting your wealth and consuming conspicuously is no longer frowned upon. From using a smartphone, flashing a Swiss watch, or carrying a designer bag, to drinking expensive coffee, what was once reserved for the upper elite is now a middle-class pastime. This inequality is most evident in Pyongyang, where people cannot help but be aware that there are those who can enjoy such pursuits, and those who cannot.

Though the central government itself is basically bankrupt, government agencies and elite officials are engaged in all manner of profitable enterprise. Trade with China, one of the main wealth creators, has risen from around US$500 million annually in 2000 to US$6 billion in 2013. So, in spite of the decline of Chongryon, new buildings are springing up all over Pyongyang, along with new restaurants, shops, and leisure facilities for the upper class and newly-emerging entrepreneurial class. Though the capital still may compare with a mere third-tier Chinese city in terms of development, the fact that one can go to a (quasi) privately-owned restaurant or cafe, order a pizza or a green tea latte and see people using iPads, will come as a surprise to those who consider North Korea to be a universally impoverished, communist country.

The Mercedes, BMW, and Lexus cars imported into North Korea are not merely for the Kim family. Many government officials possess such vehicles, and usually favor black ones with tinted windows. Those of high rank can easily be discerned by their licence plates, which begin with "7.27." But there are also plenty of rich Pyongyang businessmen (and indeed, North Koreans doing business in China) who own luxury foreign cars. There are indeed self-made millionaires in the capital who can afford to drive Lexuses brought in from China and sold at inflated prices; according to a source, there is even one entrepreneur who has built a net worth of more than US$10m, despite not being related to the Kims or any other elite family. He is simply a member of the emerging capitalist elite who managed to play the new public-private game well.[31]

But for the millions of North Koreans who live a hand-to-mouth existence, the idea of driving a BMW and living in a Mansudae apartment is beyond even imagination. In the countryside, farmers still plow the fields with oxen. Soldiers subsist on gruel. And even in the more ordinary districts of Pyongyang, there are hundreds of thousands of people living in poverty. The standard of living of the average North Korean is probably worse than it was in the 1970s. It is natural to assume that the rise of the new Pyongyang rich will add a layer of in-

31. What political impact could such developments have? While new business elites may have their own political agendas, it is also important to remember that their privileged position depends upon regime approval and regime connections. North Korea's new rich are essentially business partners with the state, and will therefore be wary of rocking the boat. What is truly required is a large, emerging middle class.

sult to injury for the poor masses.

Members of the core North Korean leadership are surely aware of this. They are also aware of the potentially disruptive effects of capitalism over their ability to maintain control in the long run. But equally, they know they cannot eradicate markets, as an end to private trade would mean total economic failure and a new famine, threatening the very survival of the state. At the same time, public-private capitalism also allows the leadership to build patronage and loyalty in an era where ideology no longer matters.

Of course, nobody truly knows what economic future the regime leadership intends for North Korea. And it is, in fact, difficult to speak of "the regime" as an organization with a single goal, because it is heavily factionalized. But if we accept that the one thing each faction has in common is the desire for the survival of the system, a reasonable guess may run as follows: the DPRK will allow capitalism and economic reform to develop at the minimum necessary pace required to head off long-term collapse—whilst resisting more rapid change, for the exact same reason.

This explains the lure of the Special Economic Zone. With an SEZ, one can generate hard cash whilst maintaining a firm grip on the rest of the country. It therefore makes understandable why the Kim Jong Un administration announced in November 2013 that it would create 14 new SEZs, a very large number for such a small country. Until now, existing SEZs, like the Rason Special Economic Zone, have failed to live up to expectations. But that will not stop future efforts to generate cash without embracing socio-political change.

With marketization, the leadership is walking a tightrope. Adapting too slowly—or too quickly—could have fateful consequences for the regime. However: we should be careful not to be too easily seduced by the "collapsist" school of Pyong-yangology. The DPRK has already survived the fall of the Soviet Union, a devastating famine, and the abject failure of its own economic system. Economically, North Korea is a modern-day Wild West, but political control is a different story, especially in the capital. The Kims and their associates still hold some very powerful cards. Patronage, fear of punishment, propaganda, a certain amount of residual respect for Kim Il Sung, and the seductive power of monarchy—for that is what the DPRK is—all strengthen their hand.

Chapter 2

Leisure Time in North Korea

B ased on the popular image of the DPRK, one may consider the idea of "having fun in North Korea" mere black comedy. Life is, indeed, hard for the average North Korean, and the usual enablers of fun—free time and disposable income—are in short supply. In South Korea, everyone machine-washes their clothes; an excellent road and rail network means that anywhere in the country is within easy reach and people have money to spend on a seemingly endless range of diversions. None of these things are true of North Korea. South Koreans are also not required to attend "self-criticism" sessions and neighbourhood meetings on a regular basis, as their Northern cousins are.[1]

However, just like the rest of the world, North Koreans do still seek out opportunities to enjoy themselves. This is in spite of their tough situation—and runs contrary to the ridiculous international media image that suggests that DPRK citizens are robots who simply live to serve their "Dear Leader." More-

---

1. Though having said that, South Koreans do work exceptionally long hours. And increasingly, North Koreans are shirking off from neighbourhood meetings, a result of the weakening of control at the local level.

over, as a result of recent technological changes, North Koreans are finding a few more ways to have fun than before. Some of those changes are even beginning to affect the government's ability to control the people.

Foreign TV and Movies

One of the more benign things Kim Jong Il was known for was his love of cinema. He had a personal collection of thousands of movies. Kim was also a fan of South Korean television—particularly that of national broadcaster KBS. When members of South Korean President Roh Moo-hyun's entourage asked Kim Jong Il why he liked KBS during a summit in 2007, the dictator replied, "I'm accustomed to state-owned things."

However, Kim Jong Il did not extend the privilege to the rest of his countrymen. The consumption of foreign media is punishable by law in the DPRK. But that does not mean that nobody consumes it. According to a 2010 survey,[2] around half of 250 North Korean defectors questioned said they had seen foreign television or movies, and many officials in Pyongyang will privately admit the same.[3] Four percent had even directly tuned into KBS television from North Korea. Furthermore, all of those who said they had tuned in also claimed to be regular viewers, suggesting that KBS is very attractive to those North Koreans able to receive the signal.

The survey focused disproportionately on those from the

---

2. Intermedia, "A Quiet Opening: North Koreans in a Changing Media Environment" (report published 2012)
3. In fact, officials are more likely than anyone else to be watching foreign media. They have more money, a greater likelihood of escaping punishment, and in the case of State Security Department officers, access to confiscated materials

north of North Korea—particularly North Hamgyong Province, since there are a high number of defectors from there—and so the result is actually likely to underestimate the popularity of directly-accessed South Korean television in the DPRK. Why? Because only those living within 50–75 miles of South Korea are able to pick up the signal, with the range depending upon atmospheric conditions.[4] People in places like Kaesong or Sari-won (both not so far from the border) may tune in, but those from Hamgyong generally cannot.

Though northern North Koreans cannot directly tune into KBS, they can, however, watch South Korean shows beamed in from China. The border region around North Korea has a large Korean population, so stations like Yanji TV do broadcast Korean language content. Eighteen percent of those North Korean defectors surveyed said they had seen Yanji TV from inside the DPRK, with 15 percent adding they had watched it on a weekly basis. To illustrate how relatively boring state television is, 51 percent of those surveyed said they had seen North Korean channels—a unsurprisingly high figure considering that it has the advantage of being legal—but only 14 percent said they had watched it weekly.[5]

---

4. Signal jamming is also less of an issue than one might assume. Jamming requires a lot of electricity, a luxury North Korea does not possess. Thus jamming is usually only employed at sensitive times, i.e., in the aftermath of the death of Kim Jong Il. Radio propagation, i.e., atmospheric conditions, also makes jamming shortwave radio signals difficult, meaning the radios themselves become a prohibited item. Anti-North Korean radio programs are broadcast over shortwave via radio towers in western Seoul, although the South Korean government does not officially recognize their existence.

5. Whilst almost every North Korean has at some point consumed state media, most, especially young people, do not really tune in when there is nothing to be gained from watching it. North Koreans describe state media as "stale" or "obvious." These are labels that most foreigners might

Television and radio sets sold in North Korea come with presets tuned to state-owned broadcasters like Korean Central Television (KCTV), the Korean Educational and Cultural Network, or the Pyongyang-only Mansudae TV. A TV set legally sold in North Korea cannot access anything else—unless one is prepared to break the law and tamper with it. And furthermore, North Korean TV is broadcast using the PAL video system, unlike the NSTC used by South Korea. But North Koreans are nothing if not resourceful (and inevitably so, given their tough circumstances), so a thriving illegal business in "modding" TVs and radios has developed. Television repairmen in North Korea are able to earn a profitable living. There are also plenty of people who watch on Chinese sets made for both PAL and NSTC systems.

Direct reception of Chinese or South Korean television is dwarfed by the importation of movies and TV series via China, on both DVD and USB memory sticks. The DVD became commonplace in North Korea in the mid-2000s, and since roughly 2010, the USB stick has taken off and, in some cases, taken over—thanks in part to its small size, which is easy to conceal from the watchful eyes of State Security Department agents. The former has already had an effect on the state's control of information, but it is the latter which, as we shall see, has the greater potential to bring change.

Chinese-Korean[6] traders with good connections bring in pirated DVDs of American, South Korean, and Chinese mov-

---

apply to the South Korean dramas which are secretly popular in North Korea not just for the glimpses of the outside world that can be gained from watching them, but because they are genuinely compelling and relatable compared to what's shown on state television.

6. Similarly, *Chosunjok* (ethnic Korean citizens of China) can also be seen doing business in places like Rason. They, too, are a source of foreign media.

ies and television shows—perhaps several thousand discs at a time. They may have to bribe officials with two or three hundred. Then they sell the rest to wholesalers in border towns like Hyesan; the wholesalers then resell them at a profit to smaller *jangmadang* traders. These wholesalers need regime connections, due to the fact that their business is not merely illegal, but also undermines state control over information. Punishment is consequently much more severe. Ordinary traders therefore do not engage in DVD wholesaling unless they have a very high tolerance of risk, or the means to pay large bribes.

DVDs ultimately reach the *jangmadang* at an equivalent price of less than US$1 per disc, and are bought by a surprisingly wide range of people. As the product is illicit, one may apparently euphemistically ask the seller if she has *jaemi-ingnun-geot* ("something interesting"), as though one were talking to a drug dealer. And as with television, most people will have trusted friends or family members they can watch with, even if they do not possess their own DVD player. Many do watch DVDs of North Korean shows, of course, but it is foreign content that has become the real draw. Around half the population has watched a foreign DVD.

But in an era where computer ownership is also growing rapidly, North Koreans are now increasingly likely to seek out video files delivered by USB stick as well. In fact, some say that this method has started to replace the DVD. Many North Koreans are now sharing USB sticks loaded with video files of foreign movies and TV shows, and as one may expect, pornography. The USB stick has certain major advantages over a DVD. First of all, the contents of a USB stick can be endlessly copied and distributed. They are also safer. One old method the authorities used to crack down on viewers of foreign TV and movies was to cut the electricity to a building, and then sweep through it, prizing open DVD players to see what people were watching. Of course, one cannot easily remove a disc if the player is not switched on. But tiny USB sticks can simply be removed in a second, and easily hidden.[7]

Due to the decline in genuine loyalty to the regime, the viewing of foreign TV and movies now goes largely unpunished. That is to say, the typical official who catches someone watching illicit media will simply want to extract a bribe and then go on his way. Those who watch foreign media do risk being sent to prison camps, but more often than not they will simply end up handing over cash to officials if caught.[8] The rapid growth of DVD and USB content delivery means that authorities cannot even hope to monitor viewers effectively.

This, in turn, is emboldening the populace. Those who defected three or four years ago may state that they watched foreign content alone, but these days, North Koreans are watching with close friends and family members (albeit with the doors locked, and the curtains closed). People are also less likely to inform on each other today.[9] In fact, it is common to hear of

---

7. Micro SD cards, about the size of a fingernail, are even easier to conceal and can be easily played on a variety of devices using a simple USB adapter. DVD players coming in from China also have USB ports on them so no computer is needed to view the content on the sticks. Portable DVD players from China called "notel" which cost around US$50 are also popular due to their small size, internal battery and USB port— all of which help overcome problems of power cuts and surveillance. And, if you're rich enough to afford a flat screen TV, many of those have USB ports in too – meaning the authorities are now reportedly destroying the infra red receiver on such TVs, rendering the USB feature inaccessible by remote control.

8. The bribe paid will depend upon the relative wealth and status of the person caught. Naturally, those with more money will have to pay bigger bribes. This bribe will most likely be paid in foreign currency.

9. Following the entrenchment of Kim Il Sung's rule, it was reasonably

North Koreans excitedly discussing South Korean dramas with friends, and even neighbors. Giveaway South Korean-style expressions like *dangyeon haji* ("of course") are reportedly creeping into the North Korean lexicon,[10] creating an illicit thrill when two fans come to recognize each other through their mutual understanding of the phrase. People form firm friendships through South Korean TV fandom—discussing it with another person is an act of trust, so it enables quick bonding.

The South Korean gangster movie *Chingu* ("Friend") was an underground hit in Pyongyang, particularly among school-age members of elite families. Set in the south coast city of Busan, *Chingu's* dialog is full of dialect[11] phrases, including one notoriously ribald line that refers to a female character's alleged sexual excitement. That line apparently became popular among teenage boys in Pyongyang.

Just like in South Korea, the most popular shows are drama series,[12] which typically feature storylines built around love triangles, family strife, and beautiful (but poor) women mar-

---

common for even family members to inform on one another. These days, this is much less likely to occur.

10. Even some English loanwords popular in South Korea, like "stress," are becoming common. One state-owned pharmaceutical in the North firm offers medicine for "stress." Other times though, unusual loanwords separate North from South: Both North and South Koreans call "ice-cream" by its English name, but Northerners more commonly refer to it as "Eskimo," after a famous local brand.

11. North Korean dialect can sometimes be heard on South Korean television, too. *Ije Mannareo Gamnida* ("Now Going To Meet…") is a talk show where the guests are female defectors from the DPRK. Some state that this show has made its way to the North via USB sticks and DVD. If this is the case, it would represent one of the best possible adverts for defection.

12. One popular example in North Korea would be *Gyeoul Yeonga* (Winter Sonata), which starred leading "Korean Wave" actor Bae Yong-joon. One defector reports, "I thought I was the only one, but I later found out that everyone had seen it."

rying sons of *chaebol* conglomerate fathers, and feature a tendency for protagonists to die tragically. To South Koreans, drama shows are cathartic, or escapist; they do not so much reflect real life as exaggerate it for emotional effect. But North Koreans praise South Korean drama for its relative realism. North Korean television very rarely shows the bad going unpunished, or the good losing out in the end. A North Korean drama hero will be a model worker who eventually gets his just reward. This is neither believable nor interesting.

But what can be inferred from these developments? First of all, the rapid growth in viewership of South Korean and other foreign TV shows and movies may be forcing the government to up its game. North Korean TV news now looks late twentieth century, in having proper graphics and better sets. Furthermore, sources state that more diverse foreign movies are now available on North Korean TV. Chinese and Russian movies (dubbed into Korean) have always been a fixture on TV schedules, but now, they sometimes compete for airtime with Bollywood movies, for instance. Even the British movie *Bend It Like Beckham* was shown on state TV in 2010.

More importantly, the foreign TV mini-revolution is undermining state control. Until the mid-1990s, the government had a near-monopoly over the dissemination of information in North Korea, with the only alternative source being by rumor.[13] In the past, North Koreans were told that South Koreans were poorer than they were.[14] Since almost everyone in North Ko-

---

13. People in Pyongyang heard about the Tiananmen Square massacre of 1989 via rumors. There was certainly no reliable source of information about the incident, and it is likely that those living outside Pyongyang simply had no idea what had happened.

14. And in return, South Korean propaganda in the military dictatorship era portrayed North Koreans as devils with horns and tails.

rea now knows that this is utterly false (thanks to South Korean TV), this message has been discarded. In its place is an even greater insistence that South Koreans are "puppets" of America. The "puppet" characterization is an old one, but it has gained a new lease of life in the digital information age.

Foreign TV and film is also changing the way the United States is viewed by North Koreans. Propaganda has historically shown Americans as unequivocally evil people, whose sole intention is to colonize the world and destroy countries that resist—countries like the DPRK. Posters show American soldiers grinning psychotically as they point bayonets at Korean babies, with their terrified mothers unable to do anything but watch in horror.[15] But times are changing—many defectors report having moderated their views of Uncle Sam, having seen Hollywood movies, like the ubiquitous *Titanic*, whilst still in North Korea.

From surveys and discussions with North Koreans, it appears that today, a great many people trust foreign media more than the bluntly propagandized state media. This is even the case for loyal Pyongyangites, who do not harbor serious thoughts of defection. In the case of defectors, many say that foreign TV and movies helped make it easier for them to leave, preparing them practically and emotionally. Some even say it provoked a curiosity in the outside world to the extent that it was a decisive factor in making them want to leave North Korea.

The growth of USB technology may well accelerate the pace of change. Humble USB sticks allow for the rapid dissemination of media files; they can be passed around easily and re-used

---

15. Interestingly, DPRK propaganda used to refer to *Mi-Yeong Jegukjuui* (US-UK Imperialism), but Britain was taken out of this alternative axis of evil following the normalization of diplomatic relations.

again and again; and, they are easily concealed, as noted above. In a country whose people lack internet access, USB data storage has the potential to act as a kind of substitute internet in which digital information is passed hand-to-hand. As the computer inexorably makes its way into more North Korean households, its ability to undermine state control will only increase.

It is very important to note, however, that the post-famine information mini-revolution has not as yet provoked increased hatred of the regime, or a desire for regime change. It would no doubt be tempting to leap to such conclusions, but supporting evidence is in short supply. One obvious reason for this is the fact that outside views of North Korea are limited, so there is little to contradict the official DPRK line. Even South Korean television contains relatively little North Korea-related content, since the average South Korean is mostly uninterested in the situation north of the DMZ. Generally, what portrayals do exist tend to either be behind the times, or risibly wide of the mark (witness the James Bond[16] movie *Die Another Day*), harming their credibility. One may speculate what the results may be if the frequency and quality of North Korean news coverage and fictional portrayals were improved.

Although it may seem counter-intuitive from an outside perspective, it is important to note that most North Koreans do not yet seem to blame the regime itself for the problems their country faces. Those who work with large numbers of defectors sometimes observe that North Koreans do not tend to hate the leadership until after they defect. And even then, whilst most express negative feelings towards the government and regime after defecting, that does not necessarily extend to

16. And, in fact, there are plenty of North Koreans who have seen James Bond movies.

negative feelings towards the country itself. As we should expect, most defectors miss their hometowns, friends and family left behind and even things like the food they grew up eating. Korean cuisine varies by region, and there is even a quiet smuggling trade bringing certain North Korean foodstuffs to defectors in the south.

For the majority of North Koreans, the act of watching South Korean TV and movies is not a political act. They do it for entertainment purposes, in a land that offers precious little entertainment of its own.[17] The fact that it is delivered in the same language makes it even more attractive. As people become acquainted, though, their attitudes to the outside world do change, and some even decide that they would like to see it for themselves. But the possibility of foreign media encouraging North Koreans to somehow rise up in large numbers against Kim family rule remains a long way off.

Reading and Comic Books

In both countries, people tend to see reading as something associated with study; the most commonly read books are textbooks, which facilitate the passing of exams. Youngsters in both nations study traditional subjects such as science and mathematics, but North Korean children are also made to learn heavily propagandized biographies of Kim Il Sung and Kim Jong Il. Serious literature fans do exist, but their access to material is limited by censorship and a lack of money. Those wealthy

---

17. And, indeed, South Koreans are proving masters at the business of entertainment. South Korean drama series and "K-pop" have swept across Asia as part of a phenomenon known as *Hallyu*. North Koreans may have fallen for cultural products from the South, but so have Thais, Chinese, Vietnamese, and many others.

enough to own a collection of books (and who have an intellectual bent) will probably be familiar with a handful of classic Russian and English writers. Tolstoy, Dostoevsky, Shakespeare, Austen, and Dickens are among the most read. Thomas Hardy's novel, *Tess of the D'Urbervilles*, with its theme of peasantry threatened by capitalist industrialization, has also proved a popular novel for discussion amongst university students.

There is one widely popular form of reading material, though: the comic book. Just as there is *manga* in Japan and its cognate *manhwa*[18] in South Korea, North Koreans also enjoy a good *kurimchaek* ("picture book"). *Kurimchaek* are available in all towns and cities, at portable bookstalls called *chaekmaedae*. These stalls began to appear in the mid- to late-2000s, and are yet another example of the emerging public-private capitalism of North Korea.

Chaekmaedae are organized by government libraries and publishing houses. They offer plenty of innocent love stories, but mainly, the emphasis is on propaganda. However, unlike more serious books offering an often distorted view of Korean history or the ruling family, *kurimchaek* propaganda is entertaining—and this makes all the difference. The stories typically depict war, spies who infiltrate Washington, D.C. or Seoul, or David versus Goliath[19] type battles (which serve as allegories for the DPRK's stand against the United States). Others, such as the old classic, *Sonyon Jangsu* (The Boy Commander), deal with Korea's struggle for independence from Japan. These tales are genuinely enjoyed by the public, and as such, *kurimchaek*

---

18. North Korean comic books sold to foreigners are also sometimes referred to as *manhwa*—particularly those that are aimed at Southerners—and strive to present a North Korean version of Korean history.

19. Industrious, collectivist bees defeating nasty imperialist wasps is a well-known example.

are among the more effective and subtle means of propaganda available to the North Korean government.

Chaekmaedae offer comic books for rent or sale, but a lack of money means the average customer prefers to rent. Like any other street hawker, those running the *chaekmaedae* take advantage of busy areas to turn a profit, offering low-cost products. Particularly favored locations include outside schools and universities, where teenagers (the main target customer group) hang out. Train stations are also popular, as North Korean trains are notorious for arriving extremely late, unannounced, or not at all. Bored travelers find *chaekmaedae* a godsend, as that hoary old line, "at least he made the trains run on time," certainly did not apply to Kim Jong Il. In the busy university districts of Pyongyang, students are known to slip out between classes to *chaekmaedae* near the university gates to sit down and spend precious free time flicking through the latest spy story or tale of military history before returning to lectures.

A typical *chaekmaedae* has a fairly substantial offering of the latest or most popular (and correspondingly well-thumbed) comic books laid flat along the top of a mobile wooden bench or table. The colorful and graphic covers of the *kurimchaek* catch the eyes of customers, just as magazines on stalls in Tokyo or Hong Kong do. Some *chaekmaedae* also offer e-books for sale or rent; these are carried on small USB drives—another indication of North Korea's changing times. Buying a *kurimchaek* can cost as much as 1,000 won, so most prefer to rent them for around 100 won a time (less than 2 US cents at the black market exchange rate). Most customers stand next to the comic book stall, quickly scanning the high-contrast and lively images on the covers. Some public libraries also offer the service.

The *chaekmaedae* are staffed by middle-aged *ajumma* who

request an ID card to be left as a deposit with the rental fee. Bright and colorful on the outside but printed on poor quality paper in black-and-white, the average *kurimchaek* is roughly equivalent in size to an A6 piece of paper, and easily folded in half to make it easier to quickly scan the graphic panels before the allotted rental time is up. Some North Koreans proudly boast of being able to read an entire edition in 10–15 minutes when in a hurry.

Although there are plenty of conventional bookshops in North Korea, book ownership is normally considered a luxury. The emergence of the *chaekmaedae* is therefore significant: it means that domestic literature is reaching a much wider audience. This serves as a reminder that not all capitalistic changes taking place in North Korea today will necessarily have negative implications for the regime. There is, however, growing but incomplete evidence to suggest that some *chaekmaedae* may also stock non-ideological or even foreign comic books. Eyewitness accounts in the last few years cite graphic editions of famous Western tales like *Pinocchio* as being available in some more rural *chaekmaedae*.

Computers

It has become a cliché to say that South Korea is the most "wired" country on the planet, and North Korea the least. It is true though that very, very few North Koreans have ever used the internet. Those who have are firmly within the elite, and even they tend to use Yahoo! e-mail addresses rather than official ones.[20] Considering that the state sees information con-

---

20. Usually, an organization will have one or two email accounts, and these will be checked by the people at the top. If you met a mid-ranked work-

trol as a critical means of monopolizing power—and that South Korean TV and the USB stick are already breaking that monopoly—it is unlikely that North Koreans' internet deprivation will be rectified anytime soon, despite persistent rumors to the contrary that began in the early 2010s.

A growing minority of North Koreans do have some access to computers, though. And the government, though wary of the internet, regularly mentions computers and tablet devices in its propaganda, and encourages citizens to learn more about IT. One could compare the overall situation to that of wealthier countries in 1990: though still somewhat the preserve of the few, there is a sense that computers are "the future." And just as in 1990, the vast majority of those computers are not networked.

Laptop computers are most prized among North Koreans, and particularly by those who enjoy watching foreign media. This is because they are small and portable, and thus more easily hidden. At places like Kangdong Market in Pyongyang, a Chinese laptop will cost US$300 or more (depending on the spec). This is a lot of money to most North Koreans. Secondhand desktops are bringing computing closer to the average citizen, though, costing around US$150 each. One plausible estimate puts the combined total number of laptops and desktops in the country at around four million, or around one for every six people. Around half of those computers are in wealthier Pyongyang, though, skewing the average somewhat. There is probably one computer for every eleven people outside the capital.

Some computers are connected to intranet networks. These are DPRK-only "walled gardens," and act as a kind of official North Korean internet. Hacker collective Anonymous once claimed to have infiltrated one of these networks, but since there

---

er and decided to send him an email, it would probably never reach him.

will have been no link to the outside world, it is hard to see how this might have been possible.[21] The largest network, Kwang-myong, is free to use and is accessible from universities and government offices, as well as privately, for those with a phone line and a computer. Much of Kwangmyong's content is simply taken from the regular internet, and posted after passing the eyes of censors. Kwangmyong also provides e-mail, messenger chat, a library of e-books, news, and access to North Korean websites.

Visitors to Pyongyang these days like to play "spot the tablet." For members of the elite, a Chinese-bought tablet is both a fun toy and a status symbol. It is therefore becoming common to see young "Pyonghattan" dwellers sitting in cafes, playing with their mobile devices as they sip on lattes. The North Korean government has itself gotten in on the act, having produced its own Android tablet, the Samjiyon. The Samjiyon isn't truly a North Korean product, though. Its operating system is Android, and its inner circuitry comes from Yecon, a Chinese company based in the manufacturing powerhouse city of Shenzhen. It costs the equivalent of US$200, and according to one source who managed to buy one at a Pyongyang trade fair, it has a version of "Angry Birds," a PDF file reader, and some pre-loaded e-books. Its capabilities are comparable with most internationally known tablets—with one exception. The Samjiyon has no Wi-Fi function. Wi-Fi would be a completely useless feature in North Korea.[22]

Given its price, and the fact that any North Korean with money can now buy foreign goods, it is unlikely that the Sam-

---

21. Further investigation by the authors revealed the claim to be unfounded.
22. However, certain embassies in Pyongyang were leaving their internal Wi-Fi password-free, enabling passers-by to get online; the DPRK authorities have since clamped down on this practice, threatening to "remove" any Wi-fi equipment that "influences" the neighbouring areas.

jiyon will be a hit. According to sources across all social levels and geographical regions, North Korean products are universally considered to be unfashionable. Anything Japanese or European is desirable, while anything Chinese is considered low-quality and cheap, but slightly better than its North Korean equivalent. One could simply consider the Samjiyon a propaganda effort, aimed at showing North Koreans (and the outside world) that the DPRK is joining the information revolution.

The sight of Pyongyangites using tablets is eye-catching, but the real focus of attention should be on the PC—or rather, the PC in conjunction with the USB drive. According to a survey of 250 recent defectors in 2010, 16 percent had enjoyed access to computers. Given the previous explosive growth seen in access to television and DVDs, it is reasonable to assume that this figure will be much higher now. And as one single computer may be used as a conduit via which a potentially unlimited number of people can receive foreign media on USB sticks, the PC's potential for undermining state control of information is enormous.

The foreign media-plus-PC combination has produced another, more benignly curious, outcome. Internet cafes (or *PC-bang*) are everywhere in South Korea, and serve as networked game rooms in which youngsters can compete against each other; North Koreans have apparently seen PC-bangs on South Korean television, and decided to emulate them, and thus, there are a few non-networked internet cafes in North Korea, full of game-ready PCs. Those who play on them must play alone, though. The closest thing North Koreans have to the internet is file-sharing via USB sticks.[23]

---

23. As in many parts of East Asia, two popular games are *Counter Strike*, a first-person shoot 'em up, and *Winning Eleven*, aka *Pro Evolution*, a football game.

Eumjugamu

What is *eumjugamu*? Its literal meaning is "drinking, music, and dancing." The three tend to go together, of course, and nowhere more so than in Korea, where a combined term for them exists. Although one will very rarely read of it in a "serious" English language book about Korea, *eumjugamu* is an important part of life in Korea. There exists a stereotype that portrays Koreans as the Irish of the East; but unlike some stereotypes, this one contains a strong element of truth.

Anyone who has spent time in South Korea will attest to the joys of a night out drinking beer and *soju* (a colorless spirit traditionally based on potatoes or rice), followed by an hour or two in a *noraebang* (karaoke) room, where one may sing along, dance, and shake a tambourine to one's favorite songs. And while we now approach seven decades of division in Korea, the spirit of *eumjugamu*—which can be traced back to shamanic tradition and ancient festivals like *Dano*—is so deeply rooted in Korean culture that those in the North still have an undimmed love for it.

The DPRK's leaders have certainly been no exception. Kim Jong Il was known for his love of partying. He was a particularly heavy drinker,[24] who favored expensive Hennessy cognac—also the drink of many South Korean *chaebol* leaders. His circle was noted for its alcohol consumption, and his son Kim Jong Un appears to be following suit, if basketball player Dennis Rodman's visit to the resort town of Wonsan can be taken as representative. The pair spent three days drinking

---

24. At least, he was in his younger years. Later on, he would drink colored water, preferring to see those around him drunk whilst remaining sober himself.

도 착   ARRIVALS

편명번호   출발공항지역   도착예정시간   도착시간   비고
FLIGHT N°   ORIGIN   SCHEDULED   EXPECTED   REMARKS

TOP: Pyongyang's Sunan Airport in 2010 before undergoing comprehensive renovations in 2014. The arrivals board shows no flights, but national carrier Air Koryo and Chinese carrier Air China currently schedules fairly regular flights in and out of the country, and regular chartered flights in the summer to the Chinese cities of Yanji and Changchun. North Korea restarted scheduled domestic flights in 2014 amid ongoing efforts to boost tourism.
Photo: Roman Harak

BOTTOM: Means of transport are in short supply in North Korea so civilian vehicles are often re-purposed for military or cargo use. In this case, a locally-produced "Jipsan 82" bus, produced in the 1980s by the Chongjin Bus Works, is being used to ship beer (and not people).
Photo: Roman Harak

Preparing for Arirang Mass Games often means long nights of training and millions of labor hours on top of the usual study or work duties required from its participants—an extra curricular demand put on children not too dissimilar from the cram schools attended by children in South Korea which, like the Mass Games, is something people

struggle with and rest but also find common purpose and community in. Many participants are adults or school children, who are sometimes required to turn colored pages from a book in perfect unison to animate a giant human screen for the backdrop of the show. *Photo: Joseph A Ferris III*

TOP: Pyongyang's school children and young adults can spend hours of their year preparing for the Arirang Mass Games, a mass display of gymnastics, and martial arts. *Photo: Joseph A Ferris III*

BOTTOM: A North Korean mother with her children at the Kaeson Youth Park in central Pyongyang. Rain boots are a popular choice of footwear in Pyongyang where they are seen as being quite fashionable. The same applies in the countryside, where they are also practical for carrying out collectivized labor or farming. *Photo: Roman Harak*

TOP: A barbershop in Rajin, part of the Rajin-Songbon special economic zone. Contrary to rumors in the press, North Koreans were not ordered to get Kim Jong Un haircuts. There are, however, certain stylers to chose from—and a certain amount of self-censorship influences this. Some girls dye their hair lighter, often at risk of great criticism.
Photo: James Pearson

BOTTOM: Like metro systems around the world, some stations have small shops selling everything from toys, to drinks priced using gray market rates for the won.
Photo: Wang Hsieh

Rush hour in the city of Kaesong which was part of South Korea right until the very last stages of the 1950-53 Korean War. Its proximity to the South can make the city feel tense at times but it also makes it easy to pick up South Korean and American military radio broadcasts. *Photo: Wang Hsieh*

TOP: Women in Pyongyang carrying shopping home from the market. Sharing the load of bags is a common sight in North Korea, where bad transport links could mean moving heavy goods by foot over long distances, even in the capital. *Photo: Roman Harak*

BOTTOM: One of the most important things on display in North Korea, often contrary to the State's wishes, is market-level capitalism like this. Here women in the city of Hamhung set up road-side stalls where they sell food or products to passersby. *Photo: Lily Saywell*

TOP: One of the most noticeable changes to have taken place in North Korea in the past five years is the rise of the cell phone. Since the 2008 launch of network operator Koryolink, more than two million North Koreans have bought cellular phones and registered with the service. *Photo: Joseph A Ferris III*

BOTTOM: Mobile phones like this one used by a woman crossing tracks at Shinuiju Railway Station near the Chinese border have become increasingly prevalent in recent years. However, the system is very expensive for locals, and the fact it is denominated in hard currency means the vast majority of the population cannot own mobile phones. *Photo: Alexander Akulov*

A country road between fields in rural South Hwanghae province. Bicycles are used not just for moving between home and the fields, but also for transporting excess produce to the market. Note the hillsides in the background have also been cultivated—a result

of poor agricultural policy, private farm plots on inhospitable ground, and the problems of shifting soil and landslips. *Photo: Lily Saywell*

The road from the Rason Special Economic Zone (SEZ) to the Chinese border, as it was being built by Chinese workers, and Chinese money. China has also paid for a multi-million dollar suspension bridge that now spans the Yalu river, linking the Chinese city of Dandong with the North Korean city of Shinuiju. *Photo: Roman Harak*

TOP: Men fish near the port at Wonsan, on North Korea's east coast. This pier is just a short drive away from Kim Jong Un's summer palace where he keeps all manner of luxury toys, including two yachts made by Princess Yachts. *Photo: James Pearson*

BOTTOM: Days out at the beach like this one in Wonsan are a popular summer pastime for those close enough to the coast. Those without access to the sea make do with mountainous North Korea's local rivers and streams. Internal travel is difficult, however, due to an extensive network of internal borders that require bribes to pass without the correct paperwork. *Photo: Alexander Akulov*

TOP: A farm house in rural North Korea, not too far from the border with the South. Poverty and a shortage of supplies often means rural dwellings fall into a perpetual state of disrepair. *Photo: Roman Harak*

BOTTOM: A fairly common rural street scene in South Pyong'an province. A privately cultivated vegetable plot can be seen in the foreground, most likely feeding the family in the adjacent house, and producing valuable produce to sell on the black market. *Photo: Lily Saywell*

TOP: A rare advert for state automobile producer "Pyonghwa Motors," a joint-venture with a South Korean company that produces cars from Fiat and Brilliance China Auto under license. The advert says "From Mt. Paektu (in North Korea) to Hallasan (in South Korea)"— an ironic statement given the DMZ that divides North from South Korea is the world's most impenetrable and fortified border. For those with the money, the BMW and Mercedes cars imported into North Korea are not merely for the Kim family. There are plenty of rich Pyongyang businessmen who possess such vehicles. *Photo: Joseph A Ferris III*

BOTTOM: Young middle-class and probably moneyed newlyweds head to the beach for wedding photos in Wonsan, on the east coast. *Photo: James Pearson*

TOP: Construction on Pyongyang's Ryugyong Hotel began as a glory project in 1987 but visibly foundered in the 1990s when funding ran out. Still unfinished, the shiny pyramid ominously towered over the North Korean capital as an empty shell before finally getting its glass exterior in 2010, thanks to investment from a foreign company. Sources say the hotel will open in the next few years. *Photo: Roman Harak*

BOTTOM: A statue in Pyongyang shows idealized people representing the three symbols behind the ruling Workers' Party of Korea—a worker holding a hammer, a peasant with a sickle, and the uniquely North Korean addition to the Soviet trope of a "working intellectual" with a brush. *Photo: Roman Harak*

Graffiti can be seen scratched into the windows of Pyongyang Metro cars, but anything legible is in German—many of the cars were shipped over from East Germany in the 1990s. Contrary to a popular myth that only two stations exist, the Pyongyang Metro actually has 16 stations, spread over two lines. However, the line does not cross south of the river Taedong, leaving many commuters in Pyongyang's own "Gangnam" forced to commute by foot, bicycle, or bus. *Photo: Wang Hsieh*

TOP: Young teenagers hop off the metro at a stop in downtown Pyongyang. Their clothes might look quite normal but in Pyongyang they would be considered quite trendy—and maybe even a little bit rebellious, in the eyes of some North Koreans. *Photo: James Pearson*

BOTTOM: A man reads the daily publication of the ruling Workers' Party, the *Rodon Shin-mun*, on a platform whilst waiting for the next metro train to arrive. *Photo: Wang Hsieh*

TOP: Newspapers are often put in public display cases—here, on Pyongyang's underground railway system. A similar sight can still be seen in central Seoul. *Photo: Joseph A Ferris III*

BOTTOM: Curious school children peer into the lens of a foreign tourist's camera in the eastern port town of Wonsan. No camera in Asia escapes the omnipresent peace sign, not even in North Korea. *Photo: Joseph A Ferris III*

ABOVE: North Korean school children wear the same red scarves the Young Pioneers of the USSR and East Germany once donned—they even share the same motto: "Always Prepared!." Children over the age of 15 can join the organization, known in North Korea as the Kim Il Sung Socialist Youth League. Many young North Koreans in the Youth League are encouraged to get involved in social control, including acting as fashion police to check for "subversive" clothing. In this case, the girls are using a parasol to protect their skin from the sun—a very common but nevertheless quite widespread fashion accessory in North Korea. *Photo: Joseph A Ferris III*

OPPOSITE TOP: Propaganda at the Mangyongdae Children's Palace in Pyongyang showing eternal president Kim Il Sung with his son and former leader, Kim Jong Il. *Photo: Roman Harak*

RIGHT: Former leaders Kim Jong Il (left) and his father Kim Il Sung (right) are regularly featured in propaganda images standing atop Mt. Paektu, a mountain on the border with China. *Photo: Roman Harak*

TOP: A man pushes his wife in a handcart in the city of Hamhung, North Korea's second-largest city. Handcarts are widely used in North Korea to move goods or, on occasion, people too. Bicycles are also extremely popular, although not always available without the money or the means to get one. *Photo: Joseph A Ferris III*

BOTTOM: Handcarts like these are often used to move goods between home and the market, and can still be seen being used by elderly workers in South Korea. *Photo: Roman Harak*

TOP LEFT: Bicycles like the one this lady is using in the town of Munchon, South Hamgyong Province are useful for transporting things either to or from the market. However, poorly maintained roads in North Korea often mean one of the most popular private service jobs is bicycle repair. *Photo: Alexander Akulov*

TOP RIGHT: Tricycles like this one used by a rural North Korean in North Hwanghae province are also useful for moving goods between towns, villages, markets and farms. China's traffic-heavy roads were also once totally dominated by bicycles. On a similar note, a popular status symbol in North Korea for those with the money to purchase and maintain one is the motorcycle—many of which are brought in from China. *Photo: Lily Saywell*

BOTTOM: It is still an unimaginable dream for the ordinary citizen to purchase a car, but some elite can afford even the most opulent of cars, such as this Hummer spotted by a foreign tourist in Pyongyang. North Koreans who know what such a car is have been known to quietly disapprove of such a gas-guzzling vehicle in a country suffering from chronic fuel shortages. *Photo: Roman Harak*

Mass dances like this one are often held to mark special occasions in Pyongyang. It might be forced fun, but some people enjoy such dances, despite the stern-looking faces state media often shows. *Photo: Wang Hsieh*

ABOVE: School children—like this girl who took a break between sets at a school in Chongjin—are often used in performances either for domestic or foreign tourist consumption.
Photo: Alexander Akulov

RIGHT: Girls in traditional Korean clothing on their way back from bowing beneath giant statues of former leaders Kim Il Sung and Kim Jong Il—a compulsory and ideological ritual required to be performed by most North Koreans on state occasions.
Photo: Roman Harak

LEFT: A little girl in Pyongyang. The first word on the propaganda poster behind her says *suryongnim* which literally means "leader" but in North Korea is a word reserved for founding (and "eternal") president Kim Il Sung. Much propaganda is hand-painted by state artists—a cheap alternative to mass printing.
Photo: Wang Hsieh

LEFT: North Korean soldiers leaving Pyongyang after a military parade marking the 100th birthday of deceased president Kim Il Sung. The average North Korean soldier is exploited for his labor, poorly trained, and poorly fed.
Photo: Joseph A Ferris III

LEFT: Soldiers parade on July 27 for the "day of victory" in North Korea, marking the end of the 1950-53 Korean War. State and international media often shows footage of stern-looking soldiers goose-stepping their way through Pyongyang, but just a few blocks round the corner the scene is more relaxed, and jubilant. *Photo: Wang Hsieh*

BELOW: Soldiers parade on July 27 for the "day of victory" in North Korea, marking the end of the 1950-53 Korean War. The number 727, taken from this date, is also used on the number plates of cars driven by the upper elite. Kim Jong Un smokes "727" cigarettes. *Photo: Wang Hsieh*

LEFT: A Korean People's Army (KPA) officer in Pyongyang. Military units are sometimes little more than free labor team. If the government needs a road built, the only major outlay might be on materials—the labor cost will simply be the amount of money it takes to feed the soldiers. *Photo: Wang Hsieh*

TOP: North Korean women are expected to enter the labor force and are even enlisted into the army, where many also work as guides, teachers or even entertainers. *Photo: Roman Harak*

BOTTOM: Female soldiers hitch a ride on top of a Soviet-era ZIL-130 truck carrying firewood on a country road between the eastern port city of Wonsan and the capital, Pyongyang. *Photo: Joseph A Ferris III*

TOP: North Korea does have a select few combat-ready troops, but the average military man is likely to spend more time building things than working to crush the "puppet" regime in Seoul. Even state media often refers to them as "soldier-builders." *Photo: Joseph A Ferris III*

BOTTOM: A Korean People's Army unit packed into the back of a truck—a common sight even in the capital Pyongyang. *Photo: Roman Harak*

TOP: Beer is one of the few things the North might just do better than the South, and many bars or hotels like this one in Pyongyang often brew their own. However, for the majority of North Koreans—especially those in the countryside, and with little or no disposable income—homemade moonshine remains the only reliable option with which to get drunk. *Photo: Wang Hsieh*

BOTTOM: Some model factories have been opened up to foreign tourists, in this case the Nampo Chollima Steelworks. Other factories are not as pristine, but in some cases have reportedly started using gray market rates to pay worker wages. *Photo: Joseph A Ferris III*

DISCLAIMER: The photos shown in this section are by no means a "rare glimpse" into North Korea. They present images that a tourist to the country is likely to see–a mix of things put on for show, but every now and then something like a woman on her way to the black market slips through the cracks.

huge amounts of tequila, vodka, and other spirits, as well as racing each other on jet-skis, and traveling on the ruling family's 200-foot (60-meter) yacht. Unlike his father, the younger Kim reportedly favors French red wine over cognac.

So much for socialism, then. But what of the ordinary North Koreans' drinking habits? It is impossible for the average North Korean to afford tequila. Most will only have had state-produced drinks like *Yangdok-Sul* or North Korea's famed Taedonggang beer on special occasions like national holidays or weddings, and will probably never have tried any of the powerful fruit-based brews (such as Paektusan Blueberry Wine) that can be bought by foreigners on visits to the country.[25] Some older defectors will even say that drinking "proper" alcohol (i.e., non-homemade) is a luxury, mostly enjoyed on national holidays.

Customarily, bottles of alcoholic drinks were distributed on the birthdays of Kim Il Sung and Kim Jong Il, as well as at New Year, and on September 9th (the day the DPRK was founded). These were not working days, so drunkenness was practically a given. Today, however, such distributions are much less reliable. But since this is the era of grassroots capitalism in North Korea, there is now a growing private trade in alcoholic drinks.

Mass-market beers, such as Taedonggang, are available everywhere. There are also another nine beer breweries around the country, meaning that at the time of writing, North Korea has more beer-making firms than South Korea. The best of these is named Kyeongheung, a firm which also operates bars and restaurants. *Soju*, however, is the most cost-effective, legal

---

25. Other spirits on sale to tourists include a strong, hangover-inducing pine mushroom *soju*, and a peculiar alcohol that is apparently made from seal penis.

way of getting drunk in North Korea—just as it is in the South. It is therefore common to see North Koreans drinking it in public parks. The most well-known brand is Pyongyang Soju (which could even sometimes be found in Seoul during the days of the "Sunshine Policy" of the early 2000s), but other cities have their own *soju* as well.

North Koreans have also always enjoyed homemade moonshine. For the majority—especially those in the countryside, and with little or no disposable income—this remains the only reliable option. Typically, homebrewing will be of the most rudimentary form—corn, fruit, or ginseng, left to ferment in a bottle or jar, and buried under a pile of clothes for warmth. The end product can be consumed by the maker's family, or even sold or bartered with neighbors. This kind of moonshine has been made in Korea since at least the days of the Joseon Dynasty. South Koreans, too, were avid homebrewers until the 1960s, when the government began stamping out *gayangju* (homemade hooch) and encouraging people to buy factory-made *soju*, which was safer. Factory-made *soju* also fitted in with then-president Park Chung-hee's industrialization efforts.

In North Korea, the practice has simply continued. Homemade alcoholic drinks there are typically referred to as *nongtaegi* (or sometimes *nungju*). Most housewives know how to make it, and those who do it well become famous within their village. Such ladies will then even be able to turn their moonshining into a small business, if they wish. According to a defector quoted on a news website (and other sources in confirmation), one can double one's investment by purchasing corn,[26] turning it into *nongtaegi*, and selling it on the market.

---

26. Corn and acorns are the most popular base ingredients for *nongtaegi*. Rice can also be used, but it is more expensive, and the resulting liquor has a lower alcohol content. Few therefore want it.

There will even be some leftovers, which may be eaten (but certainly not savored). However, the hangover produced by *nongtaegi* is considered rather exceptional.

Though *nongtaegi* is illegal, any efforts to stop its production are utterly doomed to failure. Those whose job it is to eradicate it enjoy it as much as anyone else. And according to one defector, around 80–90 percent of North Korean men drink every day. There is even a popular song, "*Weol, hwa, su, mok, geum, to, il Banju,*" which can be translated as "Drink on Monday, Tuesday, Wednesday, Thursday, Friday, Saturday, and Sunday." North Korean men drink more even than their famously bibulous Southern brethren. Northern women drink much less than those in the South, but this is also starting to change. As working class women are now often the bread-winners, they have much more freedom—but also, more stress to relieve at the end of the day.

A world away in Pyongyang, the growing capitalist elite (and growing wealth of the traditional elite) means that new bars and restaurants are springing up all the time.[27] There are several microbrewery bars that produce their own lagers and ales on site. Many wealthier urban men will drink beer all night after work, just as workers in Seoul do. Imported wine, and of course the more modest *soju*, are also popular in restaurants—many of which open at all hours, and also offer musical entertainment. Whiskey is prized, and not just as a drink in itself, but also as a kind of currency: a bottle of decent whiskey can make a policeman look the other way, a professor award a top

---

27. For those unable to visit Pyongyang, there are DPRK-owned restaurants in Shanghai, Beijing and other Chinese cities, where one can experience (middle-upper) North Korean restaurant culture. Korean barbecue and *soju* are served by North Korean waitresses, who periodically get up on stage and perform as a band.

grade, or, indeed, gain a foreign tourist special treatment.

Another nighttime option for the urbanite with disposable income is the *pojang macha*, or tent bar. These orange-colored, makeshift roadside *soju* bars are to be found everywhere in South Korea, and also existed in North Korea (at least in Pyongyang) until the late 1980s. The government cracked down on them back then; but today, they are making a comeback.

Unlike in South Korea, house parties are very common in the North. Members of all social classes like to gather in one another's homes, and share food and drink to celebrate birthdays and other special occasions. In a country where public behavior is subject to a relatively high degree of control, the house party is a natural way of cutting loose. Those who have attended one will say that the amount of drinking at house parties would put South Koreans to shame. One defector states that she never had as much fun in Seoul as she did at house parties back in her home town. She and her friends would dance to South Korean and Western pop music (see below), whilst knocking back *nongtaegi*. They would connect a combined USB/DVD/MP3 player to large speakers and play music files obtained via USB drives.

University students in Pyongyang live with their parents, just as their counterparts in Seoul do. This makes it difficult for them to hold house parties—but their solution is to convene in abandoned buildings, of which there are many in the city. It is even the case that some young lovers steal away to abandoned buildings to have sex. And contrary to conventional wisdom, some students actually enjoy being sent away to the countryside to participate in compulsory agricultural labor. Though it infuriates parents to see their children being taken away from the lecture hall to do menial work far away from home, the students themselves use it as an opportunity to party every night and meet members of the opposite sex.

Among all social classes in North Korea, parties are often enlivened by one participant producing a guitar or other instrument, and leading a sing-along. And as is the case anywhere, a man who can sing and play guitar enjoys social advantages, such as the ability to impress women. *Soju* helps the good times roll, and even if the electricity runs out (as it probably will), house-partiers keep things going by candlelight.

Karaoke (known as *noraebang* in the South and *Hwamyeon Banju Eumak* in the North) machines that hold a library of songs ready for karaoke singing can also sometimes be found in the homes of those with disposable income. These machines are the mainstays of singing rooms in South Korea, but it would come as a surprise to most people in Seoul to imagine Pyongyangites keeping them in their apartments.[28] Singers simply type in a number that corresponds to a song of their choice, and an instrumental version belts out of the speakers. The lyrics appear on a video screen for the singer to follow, while friends dance along or clap their hands. Where there is only one microphone, others who wish to sing may construct a pretend mic by placing a spoon in a bottle, and singing into the round head of the spoon.

These days, North Koreans also have increasing access to foreign music. This is being made possible by the MP3 player. Cheap players are brought in from China (as well as the MP3 files themselves), and sell at *jangmadang* for around US$8. This is a prohibitively expensive figure for the truly poor, but one that is within reach for trading families and anyone else who has been able to adapt to North Korea's new capitalist re-

---

28. The market leader in such machines is a company named Hana, which happens to be run by a Pyongyang-based British businessman.

ality. Parents buy their teenage children MP3 players for educational purposes. But youngsters are more likely to fill them up with South Korean pop music than anything else.

North Korean pop songs could never be accused of being "cool." There are plenty of love songs, of course, but their lyrics tend to be rather sanitized. Then there are the songs that no young person really wants to listen to at all: those that praise the ruling family, exhort the listener to work diligently, or deliver nostalgic memories of home towns and mothers.[29] Sometimes, people even make jokes out of these songs; one interviewee talks of university students in Pyongyang singing an old propaganda song "*Nagaja, nagaja*" (roughly, "Let's go forth"), in a comical way whenever they had to leave a room.

South Korean pop is about love, sex, and break-ups—all the topics that the young and hormonal find interesting. It is worth repeating here that North Koreans are not robots, and this is why local pop music does not take up much space on youngsters' MP3 players. This happens in spite of South Korean music being illegal, and possessing it grounds for punishment. As with TV and movies, those whose children are caught listening to South Korean music will have to be ready to pay bribes. If not, they may lose their jobs, or worse. But that does not stop the practice.

That is not to say that *nobody* listens to North Korean pop music. Many North Korean songs have a bouncy so-called "trot" or *bbongjjak* sound, originally influenced by Japanese *enka*, which came to Korea during the Japanese colonial era. It is a style that remains popular among older Koreans both sides

---

29. Parallels can be drawn here with South Korean music in the 1970s. Music was heavily censored by the government, and all albums had to contain at least one *geonjeon gayo* (wholesome song), which promoted diligent living, patriotism, etc.

of the DMZ, though in the case of the North, there is also a certain Soviet influence—the sound is a little more operatic, although like its South Korean equivalent it uses MIDI sequencers to lay down beats. One of the authors obtained a USB stick containing around 200 such songs from a North Korean bus driver. Many contained endless references to *Janggun-nim*, the "Respected General," otherwise known as Kim Jong Il.[30] But if one were to ignore the lyrics, one could easily imagine many of them blaring out of an older Seoul taxi driver's stereo.

There are several well-known musical acts in North Korea. All are—quite literally—national institutions, having been founded by the government. More popular ones used to include the Pochonbo Electronic Ensemble, and the Wangjaesan Light Music Band. Both were established in the 1980s, and are named after battles in which Kim Il Sung fought. There is also the Unhasu Orchestra, in which Kim Jong Un's wife, Ri Sol Ju, once sang.

According to an article in the South Korean *Chosun Ilbo* newspaper, members of these groups were executed by firing squad in 2012. The story goes that singer Hyun Song Wol[31] (of the Pochonbo Electronic Ensemble) was an ex-girlfriend of Kim Jong Un, who had rekindled her relationship with him after Kim Jong Il—who had stood in their way by disapproving of the union—died in December 2011. The presence of Ri Sol Ju, though, meant that Ms. Hyun had to go, and so she and

---

30. Many North Koreans themselves will say they find such songs boring.
31. Hyun Song Wol is the same singer who gained bizarre international fame for a song about her life as a proud worker, the title of which was (perhaps deliberately) translated in an exaggerated fashion to "Excellent Horse-like Lady." The word translated as "excellent horse" is *junma*, a kind of noble steed, swift and reliable. In the song, she is claiming to be a great worker, as quick as a *junma*.

several fellow musicians were mercilessly dispatched, on trumped-up charges of making pornography. There were even claims that Ri Sol Ju herself was involved in pornography, and that the executions were also a way of covering that up.

In truth, however, such tales are somewhat unreliable. The *Chosun Ilbo*—which enjoys a close relationship with the South Korean government and intelligence service—is fond of running stories based on unnamed intelligence sources, which invariably make North Korea look evil, eccentric, or both.[32] This in turn bolsters the position of the South Korean intelligence service at home, especially in an era when it faces continual calls for reform on the grounds of its politicization. And because it is extremely difficult to confirm or deny such stories for oneself, international reporters simply accept them as fact, and run them unchanged. In the case of Hyun Song Wol, the authors can confidently state that she is in fact alive, thanks to a very well-placed source. Ms. Hyun is not even out of favor with the regime.

Regardless, the government appears to be tacitly acknowledging that Pochonbo, Wangjaesan, and the like, are old hat now. Perhaps in response to the unstoppable *hallyu* wave coming from the South, North Korea now has its own proper girl band, complete with short skirts and glamorous hair styling. The Moranbong Band, supposedly created by Kim Jong Un personally, has come to symbolize the government's attempts to put a stamp of glossy modernity on the still-nascent third Kim era. Unlike South Korean girl bands, the Moranbong Band

---

32. Not that the DPRK government neglects to provide them with plentiful raw material to work with. And sometimes, the National Intelligence Service hits a bullseye—the NIS broke the news of the removal of Jang Song Thaek in December 2013, days before the DPRK's official announcement.

play their own instruments. As may be expected of star graduates of a system that produces the seemingly laser-guided precision of the Arirang Festival, their playing is very accomplished and tight. They perform dramatically updated renditions of old revolutionary songs, and have even been known to flirt with American culture—playing the *Rocky* theme tune, for instance, or sharing a stage with Mickey Mouse. None of this would have happened under Kim Jong Il. Having said this, their style is more 1980s than anything; South Korean pop is twenty-first century, and the Moranbong band cannot truly compete with it for the attentions of streetwise young North Koreans, though their short haircuts are somewhat popular with middle-class girls in Pyongyang.

Travel and Leisure

For the average North Korean, the idea of foreign travel is difficult to imagine. It is both illegal and highly exotic for anyone outside of the elite or new trading class. Unfortunately, domestic travel within the country is also a rarity for many, although it is increasing. It is illegal for DPRK citizens to travel to places outside of their region, except where permission is given.[33] And even when permission is given, the terrible infrastructure makes the journey long and arduous. It is no exaggeration to say that North Korea had a better overall railway system 80 years ago; power cuts and breakdowns can make a single cross-country journey last a week. Unsurprisingly, then, there are many North Koreans who have never left their home-

---

33. Though it should be stated that permission is often given. If one has a sick relative, one may be allowed to visit them. The bureaucratic process can take around a month—unless you can pay a bribe, in which case, it may be done on the same day.

town. For such people, the capital city, Pyongyang, may as well be part of a different country.[34]

A North Korean's first train ride has therefore long been considered a memorable event. Men typically first experience it during their military service, when they are sent across the country to serve in a particular unit. If one takes a North Korean train, one will see a disproportionate number of army uniforms. There will likely be two or three carriages set aside for the military, but even this may not be enough; other compartments may well be full of soldiers as well.

However, these days, a new type of passenger is emerging. Since the dawn of North Korean grassroots capitalism, growing numbers of business travelers have been criss-crossing the country. Because cash is now king, a bribe[35] is now all it takes to obtain permission to go from one place to another. Equivalent estimates of the bribe required to enter Pyongyang range from around US$15–30 (payable in foreign currency, such as the Chinese yuan).[36] As noted in Chapter One, pretexts such

---

34. Pyongyang in particular is off-limits. To live there, or even visit it, is a privilege. Foreign diplomats working in the country often say that it can be quicker to travel from Pyongyang to Rason, a Special Economic Zone in the northeast borderlands, by flying to Shenyang in China, taking the train to Yanji, then hailing a taxi to drive back to the North Korean border. A new four-lane highway from Wonsan in the east to Rason has been under construction for years, but funding appears to have dried up. The DPRK has still not managed to connect all its provincial capitals to Pyongyang by paved highway since the end of the Korean War, presenting a constant infrastructural challenge.

35. Those unable to pay bribes negotiate Korea's rough mountain terrain, going from place to place on foot. In this way, they avoid checkpoints and trade freely. This is an exhausting, hazardous, and time-consuming occupation, though.

36. Unfortunately, the bribery doesn't end there. Those traveling by train may have to pay additional bribes to inspectors if they are carrying goods with them.

as medical treatment or the need to visit a sick relative may be accepted by corrupt officials. This allows traders to leave their work units and travel to business hubs (Chongjin, for example) and buy goods in bulk. Then they may move on to less well-connected towns, and sell their goods for a profit.

The growth in intercity business travel, and the infrequency of train services, means that North Korean trains are overflowing with people. Passengers squeeze in shoulder to shoulder, and store their bags anywhere and everywhere, even in toilet cubicles. One interesting outcome of this is that the train now more than ever presents a precious opportunity to socialize. Non-official gatherings of four or more people are potentially illegal in North Korea, making it difficult for any group activity to exist outside the direction of the authorities. The train is a notable exception, and the fact that passengers will likely never see each other again emboldens them to be more open with each other. Korea is a society that values performance and lively storytelling, and as such, there are those who liven up long rail journeys with songs, jokes, or ribald tales. More importantly, train travelers are known for sharing news and rumors, and even expressing criticism of the authorities. The latter especially would seem unthinkable in any other public setting.

But what of vacations? Traditionally, genuine holiday trips were few and far between. Work units would organize mass journeys to other parts of the country, especially mountains such as Chilbosan, Paektusan, or Kumgangsan. But individuals weren't able to choose their destination, and had little opportunity to relax: itineraries were full of politicized group activity. The only North Koreans able to just head off to the beach in coastal towns such as Wonsan (other than locals) were members of the elite. They were the only people with the free time, and the money to pay the hotel fees.

But in the era of the new North Korean capitalism, leisure opportunities are also emerging for the more successful members of the rising merchant class. There is a small but growing cohort of people with disposable income and free time. Some of them even own cars. In a direct appeal to this group, domestic tourism is now even being promoted by the Pyongyang City People's Committee (PCPC—the capital's metropolitan government body) via advertisements in the *Rodong Shinmun* or "The Workers' Paper"—the most famous state media outlet. In August 2013, the PCPC offered tickets for a three-day trip to Ryongsupo Beach, which lies to the southwest of Pyongyang in South Hwanghae Province. Places were available not just for work units, but also for individual families.

State television news reports were also promoting beach tourism throughout the spring and summer of 2013. Such reports showed large numbers of people swimming and playing beach volleyball at Majon Beach near Hamhung, and gave the impression that these were activities open to everyone. Of course, this is not true: the average North Korean still lives in absolute poverty, and thus lacks the money and time to spend three days at the beach. But the fact that the authorities are opening something once reserved for the elite to anyone with hard cash, and even *advertising* it, speaks volumes about the changing attitude towards consumerism from official circles.

Going hand in hand with this is a new focus by the Kim Jong Un administration on leisure and sporting activities. Since the death of Kim Jong Il—a ruler known for his hardline *songun* (military first) image—state propaganda has shifted somewhat towards promoting an image based on prosperity, and even fun. Kim Jong Un's pet projects tend to reflect this: the Masik ski resort is the most famous, but there have also been theme parks, 3D cinemas, and Sea World-like dolphin shows. This no doubt suits his more youthful, approachable personal style (particularly in comparison to his dour father), but will also allow him to create a defining image for himself at home, assuming the projects are not revealed to be white elephants too soon. But at the same time, there is no doubt something rather cargo cult-ish about building 3D cinemas and ski resorts in a country where wider prosperity—and even a proper infrastructure base—are distant dreams.

While one should hold out little hope for state-led prosperity on the evidence of past performance, the North Korea of 10 or 15 years hence will likely have better roads and railways. Echoing the construction boom in Pyongyang, money has been poured into a railroad linking Russia and North Korea (nicknamed the "iron silk road," aimed at eventually spanning the entirety of Eurasia), as well as two major roads linking China and the DPRK (Wonjon–Rajin road, and the Yalu River bridge).[37] Another major project is the Wonsan–Hamhung road, which is still being built at the time of writing. The funds come from Russia and China rather than North Korea itself, and are aimed at promoting business with the DPRK, particularly for the facilitation of Russian warm-water port access and China's need for natural resources. Since both countries see North Korea as a land of opportunity (albeit a problematic one), investments like these are growing in size and frequency.[38]

---

37. Whilst the New Yalu River suspension bridge now spans over the water with glittering Chinese apartment blocks behind it, the North Korean side of the bridge and the surrounding Hwanggumpyong Special Economic Zone is still empty fields and unpaved roads, in contrast to the Rason SEZ and reportedly much to the disappointment of Chinese officials.
38. Being able to one day take the train from Paris to Seoul is also a frequently referenced ambition in South Korean reunification rhetoric.

There are also likely to be more and more cars on those new roads. Regular visitors to Pyongyang and other major cities state that car ownership is visibly expanding in North Korea, albeit from a very low base. This is also a result of marketization and emerging capitalism, particularly the public-private variety that the elite are becoming adept at. It will be interesting to see if this process has any effect on the most iconic aspect of road transport in Pyongyang: the famed "traffic girl," who acts as a kind of human traffic signal. These days, even small traffic jams do occur in Pyongyang, something which would have been "science fiction" as recently as 2012, according to one Pyongyang-based diplomat. If this trend continues, they will all no doubt have to be replaced by traffic lights.[39]

Nicotine and Other Highs

Cigarette smoking is common among North Korean men of all social classes.[40] Some roll their own with pages taken from the *Rodong Shinmun* (though carefully avoiding the tearing of any pictures of ruling family members), and others choose among the dozens of local cigarette brands available in North Korea. Kim Jong Un himself is a smoker, just as his father and grandfather were. And for the benefit of hardcore Pyongyangologists, it can be revealed here that his preference is for an expensive local brand named "7.27," named after the date on which the Korean War ended. They are priced at around 300 won per packet in Pyongyang hotel shops, meaning a real price

---

39. Traffic lights are now common in Pyongyang, and many come with cameras to monitor congestion.
40. A man who smokes heavily may be referred to in old slang as a *yeomso guldduk* (literally, "goat chimney"), on account of a famous cartoon of a smoking goat. The suffix *ajeossi* ("middle-aged man") may also be added.

of around US$3 per packet – three times higher than standard cigarette brands.[41]

Probably the most well-known DPRK cigarette brand outside of North Korea is Pyongyang, made by the Pyongyang Paeksan Tobacco Joint Venture Company, a joint venture between China and North Korea established with a four million euro investment in 2008. These are not the "best" local cigarettes, though. That honor today goes to either 7.27 or another local brand named Saebom. Until fairly recently, an international brand named Craven A was also highly sought-after; production commenced in North Korea in partnership between global giant British American Tobacco (BAT) and local state-owned firm Korea Sogyong Trading Corporation. BAT originally invested US$7.1 million for a 60 percent stake in this joint venture in 2001,[42] which first produced cheaper Geumgangsan cigarettes, and then went on to Craven A.

Craven A, or "Cat" (due to the cat image used as its logo) is reportedly a brand favored by the elite. A carton of any of these top brands makes an excellent low-level bribe, and can even be considered a currency of sorts—as it is certainly a better store of value than a North Korean banknote. It is also certainly the case that members of the elite have been using their privileged status to illicitly sell DPRK-made Craven A (as well as other brands) in China.

Cigarettes are, indeed, a growing export item for North Korean smugglers. Though this is an illegal business, the cheap price of DPRK-made cigarettes provides an incentive to take

41. July 27 is presented as the "day of victory" to North Koreans, and thus has a powerful place in DPRK folklore; as noted earlier, 727 is also used on the number plates of cars driven by the upper elite.
42. BAT made an agreement to sell its share to Singaporean firm SUTL in 2007, presumably as a result of political pressure.

packs of them across the border, repackage them as local brands, and pocket the price difference. Chinese smokers do not appear to mind too much, because the better North Korean cigarette brands are actually of a good quality. Why is this? The answer lies in competition. Like all "official" business, cigarette production is state controlled. However, there are a number of competing factories, each with a variety of different brands; furthermore, in the new era of public-private capitalism, the officials in charge of each factory have a direct financial incentive to satisfy consumer demand. Reportedly, there have also been instances of powerful government organizations like the National Defense Commission using their heft to muscle other departments out of lucrative cigarette factories.

Demand is always strong. Since the year 2000, the DPRK government has sporadically engaged in anti-smoking campaigns, with Kim Jong Il himself having described smokers as being among the "three greatest fools" of the twenty-first century.[43] But Kim, too, was a smoker who struggled to quit. Kim Jong Un also has the habit, and in that regard, he at least has one thing in common with the majority of his less fortunate subjects. Some like to claim the prevalence of smoking is a result of life in the DPRK being stressful, but this would be an overly melodramatic analysis. As recently as 2006, 59 percent of Chinese men, and 53 percent of South Korean men, were also classed as smokers.

In North Korea, traditional Confucian-influenced values remain very powerful, so it is considered socially unacceptable to simply light up in front of elders. It is also taboo for women to smoke. The middle-aged *ajumma* is exempted from this rule

---

43. The other two were those who do not appreciate music, and those who are not computer literate.

(though she is more likely to smoke a pipe than cigarettes); age both confers seniority and strips away femininity in the classic Korean mindset. It is important to note that both these social rules have nothing to do with the North Korean system: until very recently, South Koreans had the same attitude. This never stopped South Korean women from smoking, though: those who wanted to, simply indulged in secret. The same is true of North Korean women who have the habit.

Do North Koreans smoke anything stronger? In 2013, the international media worked itself up into a state of excitement over North Korea's apparent status as a weed-smoker's paradise. But this proved a drastic exaggeration. As with many other countries the world over, hemp has long been considered a beneficial plant by Koreans. As recently as the 1930s, the hemp plant was cultivated in every single province of Korea—especially in the most southerly provinces, where the climate is warmer. Hemp was a cash crop: it produced the fabric that clothed around a third of the population in the summer months, according to research by Ree Jeung Haeng. It could also be sown earlier in the season than rice, meaning that fields could be used for both crops throughout the year. Even in late 1950s South Korea, around 9,000 hectares of land was devoted to hemp farming.

Naturally, this meant that country folk also came to be aware of the pleasures of smoking. After division, both North and South Koreans continued to enjoy marijuana, though not to the point where it was considered a social problem. Besides, the type of hemp traditionally grown on the peninsula was not particularly potent. Many considered it an alternative to tobacco, something else suitable for filling out a hand-rolled cigarette. Today, North Koreans reportedly refer to it as *ip-dambae*, or "leaf tobacco."

South Korea's state tobacco monopoly (today known as KT&G) reportedly padded out its cigarettes with marijuana in the 1960s, during a nationwide tobacco shortage. It was, in fact, only in the 1970s that the Park Chung-hee administration banned marijuana in South Korea, following pressure from the US Government. Former Peace Corps volunteers reminisce about being instructed to go around the country, digging up and burning hemp plants. More than a few will admit to having enjoyed a smoke in the course of their work. But President Park took to marijuana prohibition with great zeal, and even now, casual smokers will find themselves imprisoned if caught.

In North Korea, however, there was no Peace Corps. Hemp farming—and occasional smoking—therefore continued unhindered, and today, the DPRK is considered a leading producer of hemp. It must be emphasized, though, that North Korea is not a toker's paradise. The plant was always grown to produce fabric, rather than to get people high.

Interviews with defectors also suggest that North Koreans are not serious consumers of marijuana. The drug of choice is, in fact, something much more pernicious: crystal meth. Meth, known colloquially as *eoreum* or *bingdu* (both mean "ice," a name by which the drug is also known in the US; the latter is also the slang word by which meth is known in China) is a drug unfortunately suited to the realities of life in North Korea: it is cheap, requires no elaborate equipment or specialist knowledge to make, and keeps the weary and hungry on their feet— at least until they become hopeless addicts. Recent defectors will typically respond to questions about meth in North Korea with "It's everywhere," or "It isn't even considered a drug."

How did this happen? The seeds of North Korea's meth problem were sown by the state. The regime has long relied on illicit business activities (including drug manufacture) to shore up its finances and help fill the coffers of Office 39, the group that exists to make money for the ruling family. Opium production for export began in the 1970s as a means of generating cash. But methamphetamine—which was already familiar to some Koreans in the 1940s due to the Japanese army's use of it in making soldiers fight for hours on end—proved easier, quicker, and more cost-effective to produce.

Large state-run factories in cities like Pyongsong and Hamhung started churning out meth, much of which ended up in China. Japan was also an important target market, achieved via trade with Yakuza criminal gangs: the seizure of a North Korean ship at the port of Hososhima in 2007 resulted in the discovery of a large quantity of meth, reportedly enough to constitute Japan's largest drug bust at the time. It is also understood that embassy staff were encouraged to use their diplomatic immunity to sell North Korean meth worldwide, and send their earnings back to the state.

But according to researchers Andrei Lankov and Kim Seokhyang, Pyongyang drastically cut meth production in the early 2000s. Possibly, this may have been due to pressure from China, where North Korean meth was beginning to cause serious social problems. But as with so many areas of the post-famine North Korean economy, private industry has stepped in where the state no longer operates. By 2004, entrepreneurs were busy hiring those who had been laid off by state-owned meth factories, and setting up operations in empty premises. They found Chinese smugglers more than willing to supply them with the ephedrine on which meth is based.

This time, however, the end user was closer to home. In a short space of time, meth has spread throughout North Korean society, addicting urbanites[44] of all social classes. Elites probably smoke more than anyone else, though, as they have more money to spend. Several sources claim that taking a hit in front of others involves little stigma, even among respectable middle-aged *ajumma*. Meth is also used as a substitute for medicine: many people with chronic diseases who lack the money to pay for proper treatment turn to it for temporary pain relief.

In terms of geography, the drug is particularly popular in Hamhung and Pyongsong, where North Korea's meth business originated. But the capital, and every city near the Chinese border, also has problems with meth use. A media source[45] claims that around 10 percent of people in the border city of Hyesan are involved in the meth business, when one includes corrupt officials and dealers all the way along the chain.

As may be expected, meth is highly profitable for dealers. In 2011, meth sold in Hamhung for a reported US$12 per gram. The price in Pyongyang was US$20, meaning that there was US$8,000 to be made in transporting a kilo of the drug to the capital and selling it. This is a huge sum of money for the vast majority of North Koreans. As a result, government crackdowns tend to fail, because officials are all too easily tempted to partner with the dealers.

---

44. It is generally understood that usage among farmers and other country folk is much lower.
45. The source in question is *Rimjin-gang* Magazine, a unique publication that makes use of reports written by North Koreans and then smuggled out of the country. There can be fewer braver journalists than those who write for *Rimjin-gang*.

Chapter 3
Who Is in Charge?

Viewed from the outside, the government of North Korea appears as a monolith in which all power is invested in Kim Jong Un, an omnipotent boy-tyrant who threatens the world with nuclear weapons, and executes his uncle—while still enjoying the adulation of his brainwashed subjects. Internally, however, what lies beneath the uniformed and "single-hearted" image of the state is a collection of competing factions and power-brokers who jockey for political control, influence, and money.

It is, in fact, difficult to say who is truly "in charge" today. Certainly, Kim Jong Un is powerful, as are other individual members of the Kim family. But one leading theory suggests Mr. Kim, and even the family as a whole, does not hold absolute authority. There also exists a shadow power structure set up by his father, Kim Jong Il, but over which he has inherited limited authority himself. That power structure is named the *Jojik-Jidobu* (Organization and Guidance Department, or OGD), and those who consider the execution of Jang Song Thaek to be Kim's work would do well to know that the OGD had far more to gain from it. At the same time, the OGD is no ordinary organization—it is headless, and to further add to the confusion, some of its members are not even "real OGD."

Though this book attempts to describe North Korea as it is now, to understand the roots of this shadow system we must go back half a century and briefly chart the transfer of power from Kim Il Sung, who ruled the country from 1948 to 1994, to Kim Jong Il, who ruled from 1994 to 2011. Moon Chung-in, one-time advisor to South Korean President Roh Moo-hyun on the "Sunshine Policy," once told one of the authors that Kim Jong Il was "a prisoner of his father's system"—but in fact by the time of his death, it would have been more apt to call Kim Il Sung a prisoner of Kim Jong Il's system. Today, Kim Jong Un is also a prisoner of Kim Jong Il's system. As, of course, is North Korea itself.

From Kim Il Sung to Kim Jong Il

It is well-known that Kim Il Sung's emergence as leader of the DPRK owed a great deal to luck. He had been a relatively well-known guerrilla leader, serving in Manchuria alongside Chinese communists, and later in the Soviet army, prior to the end of the World War II. He was, however, considered to be lacking in education and even Korean language proficiency, the latter problem a result of having spent so much time abroad. Soviet officials eyeing him as a future part of a North Korean puppet government were dismayed at Kim's performance in tests on Marxist theory.

Kim Il Sung, however, caught the eye of notorious Soviet secret police chief Lavrentiy Beria, who recommended him to Josef Stalin as potential leadership material. From then on, he was able to take full advantage of gifts for which he is now famed—propaganda, personal charm, and Machiavellianism—to sideline rivals and accumulate power. Learning from Stalin, he and his Soviet advisers began to encourage the creation of a personality cult that merely intensified as the years progressed. Those who were a threat were dealt with ruthlessly: respected old communist Pak Hon Yong, leader of the Korean Communist Party at the time of liberation and once the most likely Korean to rule any socialist Korean state, was branded a turncoat and executed in 1956, despite Soviet opposition.

In place of the likes of Pak came old guerrilla comrades, whom Kim knew he could trust. And crucially, he brought members of his own family into key positions as well. Despite Kim Il Sung's outward commitment to egalitarianism, and his genuinely successful early modernization and industrialization of the North Korean economy, he was a feudalist and a paternalist at heart. Korea at the time was emerging from centuries of monarchy and *yangban* aristocratic rule (followed by a historically brief 35-year interlude of often brutal Japanese colonial rule), so seen from that perspective, it is perhaps not surprising that such a seemingly self-contradictory leader as Kim could emerge. If one wonders how a supposedly communist country could develop hereditary succession, one need look no further than a Korean history book.[1]

Thus Kim Il Sung's brother, Yong Ju, became a member of the Central Committee of the Workers' Party, secretary for Organization and Guidance Department in 1962, and a full Politburo member in 1970. His daughter, Kim Kyong Hui, also joined the Central Committee. A long list of cousins gained powerful jobs. Female relatives were given (mostly minor) organizations to run, and their husbands brought into govern-

---

1. And South Korea is no different: its most powerful people are the children of big men, from the chairman of Samsung to the president.

ment. Old guerrilla comrades, too, were able to establish nepotistic power bases: Choe Hyon, for instance, fought with Kim Il Sung against the Japanese, and later became Kim's defense minister; his son, Choe Ryong Hae, was for a time one of the most highly-ranked and visible government officials.[2]

It was in such an environment that Kim Jong Il, born in 1941 as the first son of Kim Il Sung, was able to rise to prominence. The younger Kim was naturally given special treatment throughout his years of schooling, and as soon as he graduated from the university that bore his father's name in 1964, he was appointed to the Central Guidance Division of the Organization and Guidance Department of the Workers' Party. Two years later he moved to the Propaganda and Agitation Department, and in 1968, he was promoted to director. It was at this point that Kim Jong Il first became known for his deep interest in cinema, obsessively involving himself in all aspects of movie-making at the department's Movie and Arts Division. This was an area in which he genuinely excelled; and according to some, he only seemed truly happy when cutting film in an editing room, or obsessing over a camera angle.[3]

For all his obvious advantages of birth, Kim Jong Il was not necessarily a happy young man, nor guaranteed of eventually inheriting his father's mantle. His mother, Kim Jong Suk—now venerated as an idealized mother-of-the-nation figure

---

2. Choe though was never even close to being "number two," as some analysts claimed him to be. His demotion in May 2014 confirms this. Choe seems to have merely served as a useful smokescreen in the aftermath of the Jang Song Thaek execution.

3. Kim Jong Il was a particular fan of Martin Scorsese, and could discuss angles and shots in all of the American director's movies at length. It is tempting to imagine a happier world in which Kim Jong Il had grown up in normal family circumstances and risen to become an obsessive but brilliant filmmaker.

thanks in no small part to Kim Jong Il's own efforts—died when he was still a very young boy, as did his younger brother, Man Il. Later, he and his sister, Kim Kyong Hui, were verbally abused on a regular basis by Kim Il Sung's second wife, Kim Song Ae. Kim Song Ae bore the leader three more children, on whom she attempted to focus her husband's attentions, at the expense of Jong Il and Kyong Hui. She and her blood relatives around the court pushed her middle child Pyong Il, born in 1955, forward as a successor to Kim Il Sung.

However, Kim Jong Il's immediate obstacle during the 1960s and early 1970s was his uncle, Kim Yong Ju. To outside observers, Yong Ju seemed the more likely successor, given his age and experience. But Jong Il, other than possessing the advantage of being the first son, had an important edge: he was more adept at flattering his father. By many accounts, Kim Il Sung had always been highly susceptible to sycophancy; as his rivals fell and his power over the DPRK grew, this tendency only increased. His food came from private farms. Officials competed to give him gifts, including houses and young women. And Kim Jong Il, who likely also craved his father's love and approval due to a childhood starved of parental affection, was known to insist on kneeling at Kim Il Sung's feet to put on his shoes for him.

The Kim Il Sung personality cult dramatically escalated from the late 1960s, with the impetus provided by the competition between Kim Jong Il and Kim Yong Ju to flatter him. As a propaganda specialist, Kim Jong Il was well placed to boost his father's reputation with movies, books, paintings, and operas exaggerating his greatness; new creative organizations like Mansudae Art Studio and Paektusan Productions were established with the sole remit of producing works that would glorify Kim Il Sung. An entire year of 60th birthday celebrations for the Great Leader was also held—with Kim Jong Il, of course, at the helm, personally writing song lyrics, directing magic shows and, crucially, being there to receive the credit.

Not content with merely inflating Kim Il Sung's reputation, Kim Jong Il ordered the recall of the memoirs of other revolutionaries,[4] for fear that they would steal any limelight from his father. He was also the initiator, in 1970, of the practice of wearing the Kim Il Sung badge that party members affix to their lapels to this day. The badge is worn on the left, in order to always keep Kim Il Sung close to the heart of the wearer.[5] Whereas Stalin's personality cult was one that emphasized the leader as the ultimate servant of the party, the Kims went one further: Kim Il Sung was beyond the party, beyond socialism, and certainly beyond any other human being. The individual who did more than anyone else to create this impression was his own son.

This extreme obsequiousness paid dividends. By 1973, it was clear that Kim Jong Il would be the successor, not Kim Yong Ju (who was also by then in poor health). That September, Kim Jong Il was made a Politburo member, and returned to the OGD as director—replacing his uncle. Kim Yong Ju later ended up serving various mere honorary roles. Kim Pyong Il's mother, Kim Song Ae, was forced into kowtowing to Kim Jong Il, by publicly praising his mother—the woman she replaced as wife of the leader.

Kim Jong Il was also given command of the "Three Revolu-

---

4. Though at the same time, Kim Jong Il was careful to flatter the old guerrilla comrades of his father who inhabited positions of authority in the government. With gifts and honors, he was able to secure the support (or at least, acquiescence) of the old guard.
5. It is also never worn on an outer garment like an overcoat. A suit jacket, however, is fine.

tions" movement.[6] These were groups of young loyalists who, similar to China's Red Guards, existed to weaken and sweep away the old guard. But unlike the Red Guards, they were under the complete control of the center. Tens of thousands of Three Revolutions volunteers participated, visiting factories, schools, farms, and government agencies, inspecting all aspects of work and behavior. They forced people to criticize themselves publicly, and encouraged others to join in. Team members were also tasked to spy on those they visited, and pass any pertinent information back to the center. Even the Central Committee of the Workers' Party could not resist Three Revolutions inspections.

Three Revolutions members who proved adept at ratting on others were fast-tracked to positions of power by Kim Jong Il.[7] They were thus highly incentivized to participate in building a climate of fear in which even the slightest display of disloyalty could result in punishments such as public humiliation, the loss of position, or even a labor camp sentence. The latter was a very real possibility, even for those high up the ladder. In 1976, Vice Prime Minister Kim Dong Gyu was forced to swap his mansion for prison camp life, for the crime of criticizing Kim Jong Il. He later died there.

Kim Jong Il developed a spy network that reached high up the power structure. Kim Pyong Il eventually fell foul of this: reports reached Jong Il that sycophants surrounding his younger rival were fond of shouting, "Kim Pyong Il *manse!*" ("Long live Kim Pyong Il"); this expression was one that was only supposed to be used for Kim Il Sung himself. Jong Il

---

6. The three revolutions being cultural, technical, and ideological.
7. The most successful person to come from the Three Revolutions movement was in fact Jang Song Thaek.

passed on this information to his father, who by then seemed to fully believe the hype surrounding himself. Kim Pyong Il thus came to be "exiled" abroad as a diplomat in 1979. When Kim Jong Il died in December 2011, his half-brother was still far from home, in Poland, where he still serves as ambassador to this day.

Even Kim Il Sung himself was not exempt from being spied upon. In around 1976, Kim Jong Il had all of his father's telephones rerouted through his own office, so that he could intercept the conversations of the man he told North Koreans to treat like a god. The mere fact that he was able to do this is itself extremely instructive. From then on, whenever the leader planned anything that would adversely affect Kim Jong Il's interests, he was able to prepare counter-measures in advance.[8] Whenever the leader expressed interest in a potential policy or new means of glorifying himself, Kim Jong Il showed an almost preternatural ability to anticipate his whims, and deliver on them.

In addition to flattery and surveillance, Kim Jong Il used the obvious power of money to secure his status through the generation of loyalty and patronage. Office 39, the organization that has earned international notoriety as the heart of the DPRK's so-called "Soprano economy," was actually set up by Kim Jong Il himself in 1974. The money earned by Office 39 supported not only the Kim family's lavish lifestyle, but also the purchase of gifts (cars, yachts, houses, gold watches, and so on) to keep underlings loyal. The growth of the organization contributed to the blurring of the lines between the fam-

---

8. According to one source, Kim Il Sung attempting to do one thing while Kim Jong Il pulled in the opposite direction was "where a lot of the dysfunction in North Korea comes from."

ily and the state, and hastened the transition of the DPRK from a nation in which ideology mattered to one in which anything or anyone can be bought—but with foreign currency, of course.

Kim Jong Il was in charge of Office 39, but the real brains behind its development was Jang Song Thaek. Jang was born to a relatively ordinary family, but his natural charm and intelligence brought him first to Kim Kyong Hui's attention at university, and later to Kim Jong Il's. The former married him—despite the opposition of none other than Kim Il Sung—and the latter made him into his henchman and chief rainmaker.

Jang realized the great financial opportunities presented by the trappings of statehood, such as the diplomatic bag. Diplomatic bags cannot be seized or searched, according to the 1961 Vienna Convention. For the less ethical, this can be a guaranteed source of easy money: first, gold from North Korean mines was smuggled in diplomatic bags and sold; later, Jang realized that opium and methamphetamine could be moved in the same way. This method, along with the sale through normal channels of more legitimate products like seafood, generated large amounts of cash for Kim Jong Il's Office 39. Money, too, was (and still is) transported in this way—North Korean diplomats have been known to carry around millions of dollars in cash.

While plenty of Office 39 money went to luxuries for the Kim family—mansions of white marble, with ceilings so high that scaffolding is required to dust the light fittings, for instance—it was also used to buy loyalty. Jang Jin-sung, a high-ranking defector, told the authors of receiving a gold-plated Rolex watch from Kim Jong Il. Others would receive houses or cars. Unfortunately, it seems that Kim's bribery tactics introduced a level of materialism and corruption that has infected broader North Korean society. One of the defining characteristics of the Kim Jong Il era was the shift from political ideal-ism to an "every man has his price, and everything can be bought" mentality.

Regardless, the US Central Intelligence Agency (CIA) had concluded by 1976 that Kim Il Sung was no longer in charge. After using flattery to gain his father's blessing, Kim Jong Il had hastened his takeover with a technically brilliant strategy that, as we have seen, involved surveillance (and the fear thereof); the gathering of wealth by any means available to create patronage; and the usurping of established institutions by bringing them to heel with people loyal to himself—the Three Revolutions teams, for instance. The cult of personality was also extended to include Kim Jong Il, as well as his father. The "Stalinist" style communism of Kim Il Sung was giving way to monarchy.[9]

How Does the Leadership Obtain Luxury Goods?

The Kim family possesses two luxury yachts docked at the east coast port of Wonsan; Kim Jong Un's suits are cut from cloth from London's Savile Row; his wristwatch is made by Swiss firm Movado. Amid strict international sanctions on the trade of luxury goods to the DPRK, how do all of the above—and so much more—manage to find its way into North Korea?

9. Famously, the 1970 edition of the DPRK's *Dictionary of Political Termi-nologies* described hereditary succession as "a reactionary custom of ex-ploitative societies… adopted by feudal lords as a means to perpetuate dictatorial rule." The 1972 edition did not feature this line.

Trusted individuals based in Macau, Japan, Hong Kong, and mainland China have acted for years as the North Korean leadership's middlemen in an international smuggling operation, coordinated by Office 39 in Pyongyang. One Macau-based businessman, who was fined by a Hong Kong court for facilitating a shipment of North Korean artillery parts from Pyongyang to Syria, simply closed down his shipping business and set up a new one under a different name (and in the same office). For years, his shipping companies kept numerous Pyongyang department stores and hotels well-stocked with a steady supply of whiskey, fine wine, and champagne.

Kim Jong Nam, the estranged half-brother of Kim Jong Un and the man who was once considered a potential successor to Kim Jong Il, has spent much of his life in reluctant exile, working as the North Korean leadership's man on the outside, facilitating the procurement of these sought-after luxury goods and the export of North Korean arms. From luxury yachts to stretch Mercedes, if it can fit on a container ship, it can find its way to Pyongyang, escaping the watchful eye of UN sanctions.

The same is true of arms imports. The United Nations now says North Korea uses complex techniques pioneered by drug-trafficking organizations to conceal the movement of small arms, as well as nuclear weapons or missile components. It has also developed more complicated financial countermeasures to mask its financial transactions from international scrutiny, using a relatively complex corporate ecosystem of foreign-based firms and individuals. In one such example, North Korea embarked on a highly unusual transaction involving a contract by Air Koryo, the North's national carrier, to purchase new aircraft in 2012.

It paid for the new airplane using multiple payments that were structured through eight Hong Kong registered companies, all of which asserted they were trading partners of Air Koryo and were wiring payments owed to it.

North Korea's embassies abroad also play a key role in aiding and abetting these shadowy companies and procuring luxury goods, or facilitating clandestine arms deals.

The Organization and Guidance Department

Kim Jong Un has inherited a system in which he is utterly necessary, owing to the family personality cult. But he has also inherited a system in which genuine loyalty has been mostly replaced by fear, and where a "court economy" and payoffs encourage infighting and rent-seeking. And most importantly (for him, at least), he has inherited a system in which one rather shadowy organization may possess more power than he does, despite being leader of the country, and head of the ruling Workers' Party.

That organization is the OGD, and it represents the summation and natural extension of what Kim Jong Il learned during the early stages of his rise to power, particularly the Three Revolutions period. Through surveillance and the re-routing of information and reporting structures, the OGD has come to be the only part of the state that sees and knows everything. Though many famous figures have been ousted following Kim Jong Il's death—including General Ri Yong Ho and Jang Song Thaek—the OGD leadership is essentially unchanged.

The OGD has existed since 1946, but its role was reinvented following Kim Jong Il's accession to its directorship in 1973, when he began to use it as the main means by which to take control of the state.[10] The OGD since then has risen to become the central hub of power in North Korea. It possesses a file on "anyone who is anyone"; it is the conduit via which the various branches of government communicate with the Supreme Leader, passing instructions down and information up; it is responsible for implementing and enforcing policy; it runs a network of spies that reach from the highest army general to the lowest provincial factory manager; it "signs off" on any government or military appointment; and it is essentially in charge of the personal security and well-being of the ruling family.

So while one may consider a high-ranking army general or minister to be powerful—and indeed he would be, within his own organization and network[11]—ultimate power flows through the OGD; nobody else has full organizational visibility. Thus, while the outside world may have been watching bodies like the Politburo, such "traditional" Kim Il Sung-era organizations had lost much of their real power to the OGD. That may have been Kim Jong Il's smartest trick of all: to shift the power base without outsiders realizing. It has been reported that he liked to say "we must envelop our environment in a dense fog, to prevent our enemies from learning anything about us." And certainly, he knew well how to achieve that.

10. Not without coincidence, Kim Jong Il packed the OGD with people with Three Revolutions team experience. The Three Revolutions movement can be seen as a forerunner to the OGD, in the sense that it was used to usurp established power and transfer it to Kim Jong Il.
11. General Ri Yong Ho, for instance, before being purged in 2012, was such an individual. From 2003–2009 he ran Pyongyang Defense Command, meaning that he knew where all the leader's tunnels and safe houses were, and how they would be used in the event of an attempted coup or attack. Had General Ri and Jang Song Thaek had the ability and inclination to combine forces following Kim Jong Il's death, they would have had a strong chance of bringing the system down.

But how does the 300-man OGD "run" North Korea today? Let us now examine in more detail the powers it holds, starting with its control over personnel. To Illustrate by way of example, imagine you are a factory manager at the Chollima Steel Complex, one of the DPRK's most important state-owned enterprises. A promotion comes up—the crucial role of party secretary for the factory. You may be asked if you are interested, or you may apply for the role on your own initiative. You respond affirmatively, and the OGD goes to work, consulting its network of informers. As with the East German Stasi, the OGD "has a file on you," one which is held at the Central Party Complex in Pyongyang. There are such secret files on at least every Party member or would-be Party member (meaning a minimum of three to four million people), and unlike the "regular" government file, which is more like a standard resume/curriculum vitae, the OGD file contains details about your private life: weaknesses for alcohol, gambling, drugs, or women; extramarital affairs; comments made ten years ago that could be potentially construed as disloyal; information about old school friends; and so on. The file is built up over time via reports sent to the OGD from any informers you came into contact with throughout your life.

The OGD also maintains a so-called "party life" score, which measures your participation in Workers' Party events, or whether you participate enthusiastically in "voluntary" labor projects, for instance. Using this, and your background check, the OGD decides whether you are acceptable or not. If everything clears, they recommend that the Supreme Leader appoints you, and you become party secretary for the factory.

But what of truly senior people, such as army generals? The same system applies to them, too. The OGD actually has two sections to deal with the military. In 1991, Kim Jong Il decreed that all generals undergo "Party Lectures," run by a supervisor who answers to OGD Section 13 (responsible for military "guidance"). This means that they are taken away for two weeks, and kept in dormitories with other generals. They are subjected to propaganda and public criticism sessions, so as to instill compliance and fear. After this process is complete, the OGD decides which of them to promote or demote through OGD Section 4, which handles military appointments.

The DPRK publicly proclaims itself a *songun* (military first) state. And while a great proportion of the nation's resources are, indeed, channeled into the military, military appointments are ultimately under the control of the Party, or specifically the OGD (which is officially a part of the Party). It is not uncommon for non-soldiers to be appointed to very senior military positions. Hwang Pyong So, a career-long OGD man, currently heads up the organization's oversight of military affairs as deputy director—and is a *Sangjang* (colonel-general, just one step under full general, though he is certainly more powerful than any general with a conventional military background). In May 2014, he was also named Director of the General Political Bureau of the Korean People's Army—the second-highest ranking military title, after Supreme Leader Kim Jong Un.

This in itself does not make Hwang Pyong So powerful. His predecessor Choe Ryong Hae held the title for a short time, and was then pushed out; sources say Choe was never as important as commonly assumed. Rather, Hwang's new title is better seen as an official stamp of approval on the power he already had.

Tipping the balance even further away from career soldiers is the fact that different military units in North Korea are not allowed to communicate directly with each other. This helped

Kim Jong Il centralize power, and protect himself against possible coup attempts. It is quite fanciful, then, to postulate that a "rogue general" could secretly gather up enough supporters and overthrow the regime, or indeed sell nuclear material to Al-Qaeda. Even talking of "reformist Party officials versus hardline generals"—as we see so often in the Western press—is not helpful or accurate, since there are plenty of people with one foot in both camps. And regardless, appointments to both will have been approved by the Kim family-OGD nexus to serve the same purpose: the preservation of the system.

Control over appointments is only a part of the OGD's power, though. The OGD has the right to issue "guidance" to all branches of the state apparatus. This basically means that the OGD can intervene in any administrative matter it wishes, as well as enjoying ultimate control over the public criticism sessions and propaganda handed down to factory workers, soldiers, university professors, and so on. Organization secretaries are sent to each body to pass on this guidance, and as such may overrule the titular boss of the factory. As if that were not enough, a covert "notification instructor" is also placed within each organization, to spy on the organization secretary and report back to the OGD. This notification instructor may simply appear to be a shop floor worker, but in reality, he is an important part of Kim Jong Il's system of centralized control. Jang Song Thaek himself was a notification instructor early in his career.

Officially, military guidance comes through the General Political Bureau, which has commissars serving as majors or captains across all military units. These commissars can overrule their generals, though the general does have the right to appeal. The General Political Bureau ultimately answers to OGD Section 13, as ordained by Kim Jong Il in 1992 in a speech to senior officers. As a result, even generals fear the OGD.

Probably the only thing of consequence the OGD is not supposed to do is issue policy. That is the Supreme Leader's job. The Supreme Leader's word is law itself, quite literally: if Kim Jong Il said to an aide, "Women should be made to wear traditional Korean dress," then the aide would note this down, and it would become policy.[12] But it is the OGD that is responsible for processing and documenting that note, and implementing the new rule throughout the various branches of the state. And when policy suggestions come up from the bottom, they come up through the OGD.

The Personal Secretariat

Finally, OGD members are heavily involved in the household management and protection of the Kim family. There are believed to be nine deputy directors of the OGD (and no director, since the death of Kim Jong Il), and while four of them have "proper" OGD roles—probably the two most powerful being Hwang Pyong So (in charge of military affairs), and Kim Kyong Ok (surveillance)—it is understood that the remaining deputy directors are in charge of the leader's Personal Secretariat (PS).

Nobody would say "I work for the Supreme Leader"—it is practically taboo to even talk directly about the Supreme Leader[13] in Pyongyang, other than to praise him in general terms—so the OGD deputy director role in this case functions

---

12. This did actually happen, though the policy was later quietly forgotten.
13. Apparently, a "thumbs-up" can be used to refer to the Supreme Leader. If someone asks, "Why do we have to do [xyz bothersome project]? Whose idea was it, anyway?" A raised thumb is all that is required to gain compliance.

as a cover, as well as justifying the huge perks given to those high up in the Personal Secretariat. Such perks include overseas travel; overseas education for one's children; and access to the Bonghwa Medical Center, a world-class hospital providing care that the average North Korean cannot even dream of.[14]

The Personal Secretariat has multiple functions: it acts as a "gatekeeper" between the Kim family and everyone else; it coordinates the Supreme Leader's schedule; and, it takes care of logistics and security arrangements whenever the leader goes anywhere. These arrangements can be extremely complicated and even unpleasant, according to one source: on the rare occasions when Kim Jong Il traveled abroad, PS underlings were tasked with collecting the leader's faeces and urine from special toilets they brought with them. This was, apparently, to prevent foreign agents obtaining Kim Jong Il's DNA profile.

Members of the PS have direct access to the Supreme Leader. This means that they could pose a threat to him, and so Kim Jong Il tended to select those with whom he shared long-standing relationships, and kept them in his employ for a long time. Ri Je Gang, for instance, joined the OGD with Kim Jong Il in 1973, and became a deputy director in 1975; he helped establish the PS, and was tasked with hiring administrative staff for Kim Jong Il. He stayed there for the rest of his life, enjoying power equal to that of any non-Kim family member. Some Personal Secretariat staff even have multi-generational ties to the family, their fathers or grandfathers having worked for Kim Il Sung.

---

14. When Korean War veteran Merrill Newman was detained in North Korea in 2013, many wanted to know if North Korea had access to the heart medication Mr. Newman depended on. Bonghwa Medical Center certainly would have had a supply.

Part of Ri Je Gang's role involved running the Cadres' Fifth Section, which is responsible for the *kippeumjo*—the "pleasure squad" of women who dance, sing, and may even provide sexual services to the leader[15] or those whom the leader wants to make happy. In keeping with his official title though, Ri also presided over the OGD's secret files.

Ri Je Gang died in 2010, in a car crash. There are conflicting theories about how this happened: since Ri had been drinking that evening, he may have simply lost control of his vehicle; on the other hand, traffic is light even in Pyongyang, and staged car crashes have been used before in North Korea to remove those who have powerful enemies.

Jang Song Thaek

Those who believe Ri's death was staged would say that Jang Song Thaek had a motive for being involved. Jang and Ri—or rather, Jang and the core OGD people, Ri included—were locked in a long-standing rivalry, according to several sources. This rivalry was sometimes expressed through the removal of those whose presence aided the OGD's position, such as Ryu Kyong, Deputy Director of the State Security Department (an organization that certainly falls within the OGD's orbit). Ryu had been gaining in power and profile, winning promotion from lieutenant-colonel to colonel-general in September 2010.

---

15. Kim Il Sung was a notorious womanizer, with a large number of illegitimate children. Kim Jong Il was more selective, and apparently used the *kippeumjo* more for satisfying his aesthetic urges. He would advise them on their dancing, what perfume to wear, and so on. In terms of his highly developed taste and confidence in asserting it, the source of this information in fact compares Kim Jong Il to US sitcom character Frasier Crane! Kim Jong Un, for his part, is considered more a "family man" at this stage, and is not given to playing the field.

Jang apparently saw him as a rising threat, and Kim Jong Il agreed to his execution in early 2011.

Jang's rivalry with OGD heads and their associates was at least partly based on the fact that Jang possessed the only significant power base in North Korea outside of the Kim family or the OGD. This power came from his usefulness to Kim Jong Il, predicated on his great ability to make money; his personal popularity; and, marriage to Kim Kyong Hui, herself untouchable due to her bloodline. Ever the canny operator, Kim Jong Il actually encouraged Jang to balance the OGD, allowing him to occasionally prune its branches with purges and dismissals, as in the case of Ryu Kyong.

Kim Jong Il had previously encouraged Jang, as leader of the Ministry of People's Security, to purge members of the State Security Department throughout the late 1990s, in order to reduce the dominance of the OGD over surveillance. He even carved out a part of the OGD, the Administration Department, and gave it to Jang in 2007—no doubt causing much resentment. But Kim Jong Il sometimes saw the need to bring Jang himself down from his perch, using Ri Je Gang to purge him in 2004 (before recalling him in 2006).

When thinking about the North Korean leadership, we should consider fiefs, personal rivalries, and the need to balance them above concerns like "ideology" and whether person A is a "hardliner" and person B a "reformer." Understood in the context of long-standing factionalism, the purge and execution of Jang in December 2013 suddenly makes a lot more sense.

So what should we make of Jang Song Thaek's downfall? There is no way of saying for certain whether it was an OGD coup, a decision made by Kim Jong Un, or a combination of the two. The OGD did have by far the most to gain from it, but also, Jang was considered to have become "too greedy" in terms of grabbing business opportunities[16] that came to North Korea—so there were any number of powerful people who will have naturally resented this. He had also allegedly taken control of the Second Economic Committee, a body which runs the DPRK's overseas arms-trading activities, as well the Kilju nuclear testing site.

If Jang had possessed too much influence over both business and the nuclear program, that would have been dangerous for Kim Jong Un as well as the OGD. This, plus Jang's monopolization of business opportunities, could have been enough to bring together a coalition of elites wishing to remove him. There is even the possibility that Jang had been plotting a coup (or at least an anti-OGD coup), in line with the "factionalism" mentioned in the DPRK's public announcement about his removal. This would have given more motivation for Kim Jong Un, deputy directors of the OGD, and other powerful individuals to unite and respond ruthlessly.[17]

His removal, however, will have almost certainly had a destabilizing effect: his personal patronage network was huge, extending not only through the Ministry of People's Security,

---

16. It is frequently stated that some of the main economic disputes were over control of sales of coal (which Jang was accused of selling off cheap to enrich himself) and clams. Obscured behind the coal story is also the rare earths trade, which is an important (and growing) source of revenue from China.

17. The fact that Jang Song Thaek *and* all his close blood relations were executed could support the claim that Jang must have done something exceptionally threatening to the existing order; usually, those who are purged are put under house arrest, sent to the countryside, or demoted. But the shocking brutality with which Jang and his family were treated may also reflect the fear of his rivals: perhaps they wanted to remove all traces of him, and ensure no-one was left to pursue revenge later. Those killed apparently included children.

but also in all of the government. Over the course of four decades, he had succeeded in building a very deep "line" of thousands of people in the DPRK.

The concept of the line is also a strong one in South Korean companies and government agencies. A rising star in the organization brings in or promotes those with whom he has hometown, military, or school connections, or whom he simply gets along well with. Over time, they rise more quickly than others, and start bringing in their own people. Eventually, the rising star becomes a senior figure, with a line of hundreds of loyal people underneath him. If he loses his status, though, everyone in his line must scramble to find a new patron, or accept a slower career trajectory. The same is true in North Korea, but with a potentially harsher downside—in the wake of Jang's downfall, any number of his old line members have been demoted, purged, exiled to the countryside, or even executed.

Jang Song Thaek's line was built in part on generous gift-giving—a practice his boss Kim Jong Il also once used to win followers. Though considered greedy by some (including Kim Il Sung, who remained wary of him for decades), those beneath Jang saw him as a benevolent patriarch. He was "the man you go to see" when you needed some money—perhaps to buy a house or car, or pay for a wedding. During the famine of the mid-1990s, some people lower down the line will have been kept alive by Jang's generosity, creating very strong loyalties. Some in the English-speaking world compare him with William M. Tweed, the "boss" of the Democratic Party's Tammany Hall, who presided over a tremendous network of bribery and political influence in the 1850s and 60s.

As a result of Jang's removal, thousands of people are now having to adjust to reduced prospects, as well as the loss of a leader they genuinely liked.[18] The shocking manner of the purge will also have instilled real fear in some of the more senior members of the line. This increases the likelihood of instability and infighting, as well as defections. Those who removed Jang Song Thaek must surely have been aware of this. Kim Jong Un was in fact in a northern town named Samjiyon when the Jang purge commenced. Samjiyon is an important place in the mythology of the DPRK, as it is close to Mt. Paektusan, where the state says Kim Jong Il was born (the Kim family apparently has the *Paektu Hyoltong* or "Paektu Bloodline"), but it is also one of the fortified locations where Kim family members and top elites can gather in times of trouble. The Chinese border is close by, and in the event of a truly untenable situation, the leader and his family would simply be able to walk out of North Korea from Samjiyon. Among those with Kim Jong Un at Samjiyon during the purge were OGD deputy director Hwang Pyong So and close OGD associate Kim Won Hong, the leader of the State Security Department.

But what of Kim Kyong Hui, daughter of Kim Il Sung and Jang Song Thaek's widow? One of the more mysterious parts of the Jang execution saga is her role in it, if any. She is part of the *Paektu Hyeoltong*, the executor of Kim Jong Il's will, and was until recently the custodian of billions of dollars of family money stashed around the globe. She had a large network of her own, and (along with Jang) was seen as Kim Jong Un's regent. So, either she assented to the sacrifice of her husband, or she lost a great deal of influence in the run-up to the event.

On this question, no reliable evidence exists to make a call either way. But what is certain is that Kim Kyong Hui spends

---

18. The main source for information on Jang calls him a "genuinely nice guy," who would sometimes break down in tears when drunk, lamenting the state of affairs in his country.

most of her time away from North Korea these days. She has homes in Singapore and France, and is believed to be living in the latter country at the time of writing. She is also in poor health.[19] Even if she retained the power to give Jang up voluntarily in November/December 2013 (their marriage had become loveless, by many accounts), there will soon come a time when Kim Jong Un can no longer benefit from her authority and protection. Of the remaining Kims, we can be reasonably certain that Jong Un's older brother Jong Chul and younger sister Yo Jong[20] are on his side, but the extent of their influence is unclear.

The Balance

Kim Kyong Hui has a successor, of sorts: Kim Sol Song, Kim Jong Il's second eldest (and favorite) daughter. Born to Kim Jong Il's "official" wife, Kim Yong Suk (whom he married to keep his father happy, whilst secretly raising a family with the woman he actually loved at the time, actress Song Hye-rim), Kim Sol Song is in her early forties, and as well as possessing the military rank *Chungjwa* (lieutenant-colonel), she has long been one of the core members of the Personal Secretariat. She managed Kim Jong Il's security and logistics arrangements,

---

19. This may be related to alcoholism, which she has suffered from for decades, and depression. Materially, Kim Kyong Hui has had a wonderful life; psychologically, she has not. Her mother died when she was very young, and she was mistreated by her stepmother. Kim Kyong Hui also lost her daughter to suicide.

20. Kim Yo Jong was officially named by North Korean state media for the first time in March 2014, during parliamentary elections (a largely symbolic process designed to put the "D" in "DPRK"—but with one candidate and forced voter turnout it is, of course, not democratic in the slightest).

and continues to work closely with her half-brother Kim Jong Un. She will likely take on the role of "family lawyer" and bookkeeper when Kim Kyong Hui dies.

Kim Sol Song is also a deputy director of the OGD, in keeping with the use of OGD rank as cover for senior Personal Secretariat roles. This would appear to count against the possibility of Kim Jong Un being a mere puppet controlled by a hidden bureaucratic cabal that pursues its own interests—assuming, of course, that Kim Sol Song is on her younger half-brother's side, in accordance with her father's wishes.[21]

Furthermore, we have no evidence to show that the OGD's deputy directors are united in purpose. For all we know, there could be great disagreements between core OGD and Personal Secretariat OGD members, for instance—after all, for several top OGD people, their OGD job title is just a cover. As a group, the OGD holds huge power—but internal rivalries may allow Kim Jong Un and his family members to maintain some degree of control by balancing those rivalries. And furthermore, it is undeniable that however much power the OGD possesses, its deputy directors will always need one of the *Paektu Hyoltong* as front-man.

Following the death of Kim Jong Il, the OGD has been director-less. This was practically the only high-level role Kim Jong Un did not inherit from Kim Jong Il—suggesting that he does not possess anything like the dominance his father had. The likely reason for this is that Kim Jong Il died before the full transfer of power could be accomplished. Today, myriad sources from Pyongyang attest to the importance of OGD

---

21. Admittedly, this is a major assumption. The Kim family has proven just as factional as the rest of the government over the years—hardly a surprise, given the number of half-sisters and half-brothers around.

deputy directors, and for the first time, dare to suggest that a Kim is not in proper control. But at the same time, no deputy director has stepped up to become director, lending weight to the idea that no one person really "runs" North Korea.

Today's DPRK is best considered a formally unstructured coalition composed of Kim Jong Un and his close relatives, senior OGD members such as Hwang Pyong So and Kim Kyong Ok, and any high-ranking military or party officials who have their trust.

In that sense, North Korea has something in common with other countries. The DPRK has an identifiable figurehead, but behind him stand a layer of powerful people with interests and inclinations that do not necessarily always match. If a "hard-line" policy is followed by a "reformist" one, or a "rising star" is suddenly pushed out, it does not mean that "absolute dictator" Kim Jong Un is mercurial and unpredictable. It means that neither he, nor any one other individual, is in full control.

Chapter 4

Crime and Punishment in North Korea

I t is well-known that the DPRK operates prison camps that can rival in cruelty anything the twentieth century could offer. The penal system of North Korea is designed and operated in such a manner as to make the cost of challenging the regime intolerably high. One indirect consequence of this comprehensive harshness is that it becomes difficult for any observer to discuss the DPRK's system for maintaining order in anything approaching a purely descriptive, clear-eyed fashion. The authors will, however, try their best.

The DPRK's denial of the existence of prison camps, torture, and abuse also complicates matters. In piecing together an overview of how North Korea's penal system actually works, one is inevitably going to be reliant on testimony from defectors (including former prisoners and former guards),[1] and the off-the-record words of the rare North Korean official brave

---

1. For the most exhaustive and up-to-date collection of such testimony, please see the United Nations Human Rights Council's report on the Commission of Inquiry on Human Rights in the Democratic People's Republic of Korea, published February 2014.

enough to discuss it with outsiders. One cannot see the prison camps for oneself (except from a great distance via Google Earth), and one can certainly not access reliable statistics about them.

It is often said that 200,000 people reside in North Korean prison camps. This figure, however, is highly likely to be inclusive of those incarcerated in more "normal" institutions, for the kind of crimes that also exist anywhere in the world—theft, murder, and so on. More plausible estimates suggest that there are around 70,000 people imprisoned for conventional crimes, and between 80,000–120,000 political prisoners. Despite this, all North Korean adults know of the political prison camps, and though they do not necessarily know exactly what goes on in them, they do fear them. Their role in maintaining control is thus hard to overstate.

Non-political Crime

As noted above, North Korea does have "normal" criminals. In every society, there exist young people who fall into drug addiction and petty crime; there are those who commit fraud; there are those who kill their lovers in crimes of passion; and there are those who scribble graffiti on walls. In North Korea, perpetrators of such acts are dealt with by a justice system that is extremely harsh, but not completely exceptional, by the standards of a poor and undemocratic country.

The incidence of standard crimes like stealing has exploded since the famine of the 1990s, going hand-in-hand with the rise of corruption and general decline in social trust. Bicycle theft, for instance, is now so common that residents of apartment buildings keep their bikes indoors at night. Furthermore, the current era of conspicuous consumption and huge inequality is fueling a boom in the theft of that must-have status symbol, the cell phone.

If one is suspected of stealing a phone, one will come up against the Ministry of People's Security (MPS). The MPS employs around 200,000 people, and essentially functions as the police force of North Korea, running police stations in every city, town, and village. It has a broad-ranging remit to maintain public order, quell unrest, investigate crime, run the identification card and regional registration system that ties people to their home regions (and keeps them out of Pyongyang), police the roads, and even operate prisons. It also has responsibility for the distribution of food, although as we know, this is a role that has gone largely unfulfilled since the mid-1990s.[2] Until his execution in 2013, the MPS was also the stronghold of Jang Song Thaek, and was thus locked in a rivalrous relationship of sorts with other branches of the state.

MPS officers are perhaps not as feared as one might imagine. There exists a secretly-taken video, smuggled out of North Korea and obtained by media organization Asiapress,[3] which shows a middle-aged woman repeatedly swearing and pointing a finger straight into the face of a policeman. This is actually not such an unusual occurrence in an age-ordered society like Korea. Crucially, the video also shows other citizens coming along and taking the *ajumma*'s side. The policeman eventually gives up arguing with her, and walks away. Such incidents are not isolated, and in general, it can be said that outside of Pyongyang, ordinary citizens do not greatly fear ordinary police officers. This is because of the post-famine social

2. One source does claim, however, that Jang Song Thaek, in his capacity as Minister for People's Security, was concentrating efforts on the revival of food production prior to his death.
3. Asiapress is the publisher of *Rimjin-gang* Magazine.

environment in which bribery is the norm, and the regime no longer feels willing or able to impose strict order anywhere outside of Pyongyang—except where political threats are concerned.

The reason the woman became angry with the policeman is also important. He had asked her for a bribe. Corruption pervades North Korean society, and furthermore, the MPS is an extremely large part of a very cash-strapped government. Bribery is therefore not merely a way for MPS officials to generate extra income, but rather, a way for the whole organization to continue existing. For many crimes, then, the trouble can be made to disappear if one has a little money. Bribes vary according to the relative wealth of the suspect, and the severity of the crime; a small bribe may consist of nothing more than a pack of cigarettes, and a large one may run into hundreds of dollars. Traders caught with Chinese cell phones, for example, would find themselves at the more expensive end of the bribe spectrum. The mid-1990s famine broke the social contract between state and citizen, and created a population of millions of people who would do anything necessary to survive. This provided the incentive to steal, and now a culture of bribery provides the opportunity to get away with it.

Additionally, the MPS tends to practice mediation in relatively trivial cases. A teenager graffiti scribbler, for instance, may well be let off with a stern telling off after a meeting with the person whose wall he defaced. A young family member engaged in anti-social behavior would be considered an embarrassment to his parents, and so it would probably be assumed that his father would correct him enough so that he would not act out of line again.

But what if one committed a more serious offense, or came up against a zealous policeman who didn't feel like being lenient that day? In such a case, one would likely end up in court. As with other countries, several levels of court exist in North Korea. At the lowest level, one would be tried by a "people's court," which is presided over by a trusted town or village elder; there are then provincial courts, and the national Central Court. There are formal procedures for judicial nomination, but in practice, the judges for each are ultimately nominated, if not officially "selected," by the OGD.

Trials have an appearance of fairness. There are defense lawyers and prosecutors, who each make their case in front of the judge. The judge will often find the defendant innocent, as well; this may be the result of bribery, or simply come from a belief that the police and prosecutors got the wrong person. And even where there is a conviction, it is possible to appeal. North Korea is a very bureaucratic country with a strong sense of formal procedure (even though the most important decisions completely bypass that procedure), and in that vein there is a lengthy appeals process that may even be used successfully on rare occasions.[4]

Conventional Prison

There are five types of place a person can be held in North Korea, the first four of which are operated by the MPS and are intended as "non-political" prisons. The first is the *kuryujang*,[5] or police station, where suspects are taken after arrest and interrogated. The next is a kind of remand or holding facility, named the *jipgyulso*. One may be held there while an investi-

---

4. It can also result in harsher punishment, however.
5. Although State Security Department interrogation facilities can also be referred to as *kuryujang*.

gation takes place, or before one's sentence is determined. Those who cross into China illegally before being forcibly repatriated by the Chinese authorities, for instance, are usually held in a *jipgyulso*, while the MPS decides what to do with them. A border crosser the MPS believes to be a "political" criminal—perhaps one who was in contact with Christian missionaries, South Koreans, or who intended to go to South Korea—will be handed over to the State Security Department. Those merely believed to have been in China for business or work will likely be sent to the next level of MPS institution, to serve a sentence of between several months and a year.

That institution is the *rodong danryondae*, the labor training center. Here, the border crossers are combined with relatively low-level criminals, such as petty thieves and drug dealers. Those with good *songbun*[6] (social status) who get caught using Chinese cell phones may end up there, too. And, due to the government's obsession with promoting "social hygiene," they all rub shoulders with women who dared to wear skinny jeans, or men who dared to grow their hair long. Prisoners spend "half the day doing forced labor, and the other half receiving propaganda education," according to a source. The state's intention here is to re-indoctrinate the prisoner before returning them to society. Discipline at a *rodong danryondae* is strict, and violence is common. Security, however, is relatively light, and escapes do occur.

Those convicted of more serious crimes end up in a *gyohwaso*, a place for "betterment through education" to which the convict may be sent for a fixed sentence measured in years.

---

6. *Songbun* is very important. Good *songbun* can get the accused a lighter sentence. There are tales of those with excellent *songbun* being let off for crimes that would see ordinary people executed. For more information on *songbun*, please see Chapter 7.

The *gyohwaso* is still an MPS-operated "non-political" institution, but in reality, many inmates are there for what would be considered political offenses in most other countries. A person trading in foreign DVDs may be sent to a *gyohwaso*, for instance, due to the fact that the material they sell helps undermine the state's control of information.

Life in a *gyohwaso* is exceptionally tough. Testimony from former prisoners of Gyohwaso Number 12, located at Jonggo-ri in North Hamgyong Province (near the Chinese border), reveals that food rations there are so pitiful as to be below subsistence level, forcing inmates to eat whatever insects and rodents they are able to trap for themselves. It is common for men serving time there to lose 30 kilograms in body weight. Many end up starving to death. Gyohwaso Number 12, which houses around 3,000–4,000 inmates (including 1,000 women), is far from the exception in this regard.

At the same time, *gyohwaso* prisoners must also endure forced labor. Men at Gyohwaso Number 12 may be sent to work for 14 hours per day in the camp's copper mine. Safety equipment is non-existent, and thus fatalities and severe injuries are common. There is also an on-site furniture factory, in which accidents are very frequent. Prisoners sleep for five hours per night, so the combination of tiredness and antiquated equipment results in around one death every few days.

The only consolation for a *gyohwaso* inmate is the possibility of eventual release. Unlike the inmates of political prison camps, those in the *gyohwaso* have fixed sentences, and have their (admittedly scant) rights as citizens restored after serving them. It is even possible to win a pardon or early release by writing letters to the Supreme Leader, asking for mercy; these letters go through the OGD and occasionally, a lucky individual will gain their freedom this way. This is apparently done on special paper distributed by propaganda instructors at the camp.[7] The completion of one's sentence may also be expedited if one's relatives have money to pay a bribe, or political influence.

Political Imprisonment: How it Differs

At all levels of the MPS system, brutality is commonplace. Below-subsistence rations, torture, and beatings are all standard practice. Public execution of those who attempt to escape a *gyohwaso* is considered a normal and effective means of discouraging others from trying. *Kuryujang* interrogators can do almost whatever they please when trying to get a confession from a suspect, and prison guards have the same impunity when enforcing discipline, or merely indulging in sadism.

There are, it can be noted, other countries that operate brutal prison regimes. Where North Korea truly differs is in its system of political prison camps. A political prison camp, or *gwalliso*, is similar to a *gyohwaso* in that it is a forced labor institution characterized by brutality, but it takes that brutality to an extra level, as we shall see later. Furthermore, *gwalliso* inmates are non-citizens, with almost no hope of ever being released.[8]

Perhaps most importantly, political imprisonment happens not merely to individuals, but rather, to whole families. A principle called *yeonjwaje*, or guilt by association, sees three generations of a family all sent to the *gwalliso* for the crimes of one member. Naturally, this acts as a great deterrent against challenging the regime. A man who distributes anonymous leaflets

---

7. Bizarrely, Kim Jong Il would sometimes send a gold watch to an inmate who wrote a moving letter—but still keep them locked up.
8. Inmates at Yodok (Camp 15) held in the "Revolutionizing Zone" are an exception. If they survive, they may eventually be released.

criticizing Kim family rule, for instance, may be joined in the camp by his children, his brothers and unmarried sisters, and his parents. His wife may be spared if she agrees to divorce him immediately. Married sisters would not join him, as the traditional Korean conception of the family is patrilineal, and when a woman marries, she is considered to have left her family.

Here, we can see once again the feudal mentality of the DPRK. The "three generations" idea is not communist in origin, but rather derives from Korea's monarchical past. During the Joseon Dynasty, men who passed tough national examinations were brought into government service, and given land for three generations. Similarly, sons and grandsons of criminals and political opponents were discriminated against by the state.[9]

The political prison camp system is also completely separate from the criminal one operated by the MPS. Another organization, the State Security Department (SSD), is responsible for its operation. The SSD is smaller than the MPS, employing around 50,000 people altogether. Essentially the secret police force of North Korea, the SSD carries out surveillance— including on the Koryolink mobile network, and on North Korean officials stationed overseas—and interrogates political suspects. The political prison camps are entirely their responsibility, and in fact exist outside of the realm of the legal system and courts.

The MPS and SSD are, at the higher levels, somewhat mutually hostile. Typically, when one is in favor, the other is out.[10]

---

9. Despite denouncing the Joseon era as feudal and backward, the DPRK actually uses the term "Joseon" to refer to Korea. And like the Joseon Dynasty, it is a monarchy!

10. Control of Sino-DPRK border policing has been a long-standing bone of contention between the two organizations, for instance. The border is now an SSD issue, and in the Kim Jong Un era, it is being guarded far

Jang Song Thaek headed up the MPS for many years before his execution, and led a rival power base to the mainstream OGD group under which the SSD falls.[11] Jang was apparently considered a little soft by SSD officials, willing to take as lenient an approach to transgressors as the system allowed. Though the MPS is supposed to hand over political suspects to the SSD, one source claims that the MPS under Jang was sometimes willing to simply let people go (most probably in return for a bribe). It is naturally very difficult to corroborate such claims, but two of the recurring stories about Jang—that he was relatively humane for a senior North Korean official, and that he was highly susceptible to the lure of money—would make the tale seem plausible.

How the SSD Catches You

All North Koreans are part of "units" related to their station in life—work units, Youth League units, agricultural units, and so on. They are also members of neighborhood units, or *inminban* (literally, "people's group"), which consist of around 20–40 families living in one part of an apartment block or neighborhood. Its leader will typically be a middle-aged lady of good *songbun* and whom the authorities consider reliable. The *inminban* ostensibly exists to transmit state ideology down to the people through meetings once or twice per week

---

more aggressively. Bribing one's way out of North Korea, or simply jumping the border, is now much more difficult.

11. It appears, however, that the SSD had temporarily fallen under the influence of Jang's Administration Department after the death of OGD deputy director Ri Je Gang in 2010. The Administration Department had been part of the OGD, but was separated and handed over to Jang by Kim Jong Il in 2007 as a means of checking OGD power. Now Jang is gone, it can be assumed that everything is back with the OGD.

(such as *chonghwa*, or self-criticism sessions), and to be the conduit via which people engage in work projects—cleaning the streets, beautifying public areas, collecting food for the military, and so on.

All of these types of unit, including the *inminban*, have another function: spying. Within an *inminban* there will be at least one SSD informer, as well as an MPS informer. The SSD informer is usually of low *songbun*, or has some other weakness that SSD officials can exploit. Some are recruited through payment, but most are victims themselves, in that they are forced into complying. SSD agents take them away, beat them severely, and force them to confess to their "crimes"; these can be "forgiven" in return for the favor of becoming an informer.

Inminban held greater significance before the famine. *Inminban* leaders were said to know everything about you, down to how many spoons and chopsticks your household possessed. They also still possess the ability to enter any household they wish, as they have copies of their neighbors' door keys. The post-famine growth of bribery, the increased ability of people to move around the country to conduct business, and the decline of faith in the state, though, has weakened the ability and inclination of *inminban* informers and heads to get their neighbors into trouble.

Regardless, the threat still exists, and can be extremely serious. If someone informs on you, be it from your *inminban*, work unit, or elsewhere, the SSD may decide to investigate you. According to a source in personal contact with a retired SSD member, officials hold weekly meetings and decide who to go after based upon the reports they receive. The greater the perceived threat to Kim family rule, the greater the chance of further action. Sometimes, quotas necessitate action as well; if the SSD has been criticized from above as slacking on the job, or the leadership has recently ordered a crackdown, then the risk of arrest is elevated.

If someone informed on you as having said, "Kim Jong Un is too young to run this country," or "Kim Jong Un's mother was born in Japan, and her father worked for the Japanese Ministry of War," SSD officials would look into your background. If your *songbun* was good, if you had no history of making similar comments, or you held an important job, the information might simply be kept on record by the SSD—and placed in your secret OGD file, too. If the rest of your political life passed without incident, you would probably never even know that the SSD had been investigating you. Or, perhaps five years later, if one of your best friends decides to defect to South Korea, the SSD could dig up the complaint and use it against you—regardless of whether the accusation were true or not.

If the SSD does bring you in, your life changes forever. At that point, it has essentially been decided that you are guilty of some anti-state, political crime, and barring a miracle—intervention from a powerful person, for instance—you are going to "confess" at a brief show trial, and then be sent to a political prison camp, probably never to return. The most important remaining question is whether or not your family will be joining you. This decision is also made by the SSD; there is no proper, or transparent, legal process.

The Point of No Return

SSD agents may simply show up at your house and take you—and your family, if they wish—for interrogation. One source claims that they take all your belongings as well, and store them (bizarrely, they are returned intact in the event that you are ever released). Sometimes, people are even *asked* to give themselves up at a specific time and date. One can be certain that not doing so would only make matters worse. Other than provoking fear, asking you to show up has one additional, grim benefit for the SSD: if you commit suicide before the appointment, it saves them the effort and financial cost of having to deal with you.

SSD interrogation centers are typically arranged in rectangular fashion, with two rows of cells divided by one corridor, and an interrogation room at the end. Inmates are separated by gender, and kept perhaps five to a cell. Food rations at the facility are of near-starvation level. Many talk of not being allowed to wash, or even see sunlight during the entire interrogation period (underground cells are common). A typical method of physical torture is that of being forced to sit in one position for hours on end without moving in even the slightest way, or making any sound; failure to adhere to either of these two rules results in a severe beating.

Violence and the threat of violence are major parts of any interrogation session. You may be led, for instance, into a darkened interrogation room, where an SSD agent stands in front of you asking questions. Though you cannot see them, you are aware of the presence of two men standing behind you—one to the left, and the other to the right. If your answer to a question is deemed satisfactory, the interrogator simply moves on to the next question. If he thinks you are lying, he signals to one of the men behind you. That man then beats you with a stick. The question is then repeated until you give the desired answer.

Sometimes, inmates are beaten so severely that they die of their injuries. The family of the deceased has no right to complain about this (perhaps they were not even told that their loved one had been taken away). An inmate beaten almost to death may be sent home. The attitude seems to be that it is better that they die somewhere else; if they survive, they can either be deemed to have been punished enough, or else brought in again.

The aim of interrogation is to break the accused, and then send them to a "court"—which is really just an SSD-managed hearing. A list of offenses is read out, the accused pleads guilty, and then is sent away to a prison camp. If he or she does not plead guilty, they will be taken away and interrogated further. Interrogation is so distressing that by the time of the "trial," the prisoner simply wants to get it over with and begin their sentence.

After the prisoner's guilt is announced, they will most likely be sent to a political prison camp. Potentially, they may end up back in the MPS system, as an inmate at a *gyohwaso*. In relative terms, this may be considered a piece of luck. There appears to be no procedure or logic behind such decisions; where the SSD is concerned, everything is arbitrary. The prisoner may, however, still lodge an appeal against their sentence, or plead for a pardon. It has been speculated that one of the reasons Jang Song Thaek was subjected to a special military tribunal was that procedurally, they offer no right of appeal after conviction. Jang's enemies wanted him out of the picture as quickly as possible.

The Political Prison Camp

The political prison camp system of North Korea can be traced back to the late 1950s, when Kim Il Sung, inspired by Stalin, began interning political rivals. There have been more than ten *gwalliso* overall, but closures and consolidations mean there are (to the best of our knowledge) four in operation today. We should not infer anything from this fact: on one hand, it may mean that fewer people are being sent to prison camps; on the other, executions and deaths from starvation may have led to a reduced need for camp places. Certainly, it can reasonably be said that the overall prison camp population has decreased in recent years. However, accurate information about the camps, particularly of the statistical kind, is very difficult to come by.

The biggest camp, Yodok (Gwalliso Number 15), differs from the others in that it is split into two distinct sections. One, the "Revolutionizing Zone," is for people the regime considers potentially redeemable. Those sent there are eligible for eventual release, if they can survive the conditions of the camp. They are subjected to propaganda and indoctrination, like those in the MPS system. Child inmates even have access to schools. Revolutionizing Zone inmates tend to be either relatives of other political detainees, or those who have been sent down for offenses such as tuning in to South Korean radio, or criticizing government policy.

The other inmates are in the "Total Control Zone" (TCZ), and are ineligible for release. TCZ inmates are no longer considered citizens of the DPRK, and are not even given the dubious privilege of being subjected to propaganda.[12] They are allowed no contact with the outside world, and are simply told that they deserve nothing more than death—but that thanks to the kindness of the state, they are being allowed to see out their days as prison laborers. The other three camps are run entirely as TCZs.

What does one have to do to be treated like this? Other than

---

12. Shin Dong Hyuk of *Escape from Camp 14* fame was born and grew up in Total Control Zone conditions. He said that he had no idea who Kim Jong Il or Kim Il Sung were until he left the camp.

the crime of simply being related to someone the state truly despises, there are several offenses likely to incur such punishment. The first is the defacing of Kim statues and monuments, which provokes fear of a potential uprising against the regime. The distribution of anti-Kim literature is similarly regarded. Though Kim Jong Il personally disliked being characterized as a "god" and lamented never hearing an honest opinion from anyone, he also knew that the whole system depended upon his deification.

Naturally, TCZs also contain many people convicted of being part of anti-Kim factions. Many of these will simply be those caught up in factional infighting—members of Jang Song Thaek's old "line," for instance. It does not necessarily matter whether a person truly was conspiring against the regime; more important is the fact that their example discourages others from even thinking about it.

The other class of crime is economic—i.e., stealing resources from the state. The regime considers such a theft a political act. The stealing of state resources has become extremely commonplace since the famine, and runs from the stripping of copper piping from state-owned factories for scrap, to the bulk selling of coal from North Korean mines to China. The sheer pervasiveness of the former, and the financial incentives created by the latter, make prosecution unlikely in any given individual case. But for those convicted of it, the punishment can be very severe.

Inmates sleep 30–40 to a room, in dirty shacks of around 530 square feet (50 square meters). Again, rations are starvation level (around 100–200g of corn gruel, three times a day[13]),

---

13. Tragically, however, it is true that *gwalliso* inmates are better fed than some ordinary North Korean citizens.

and the withdrawal of food is also used as a means of enforcing compliance. Torture methods such as forced water ingestion and the "pigeon" stress position are standard punishments, as are severe beatings for even the slightest transgression. Rape and sexual abuse by guards is apparently forbidden, but that still does not stop their occurrence; and, in any case, victims have no recourse to complain. Those suspected of stealing or trying to escape may be executed in front of the other prisoners.

In having absolutely no rights, *gwalliso* prisoners are completely at the mercy of their captors. Some *gwalliso* guards may occasionally feel pity for their captives, but in order to minimize this likelihood, the SSD deliberately selects "psychos," according to a source. During guard training, new recruits are encouraged to "practice" on camp prisoners, selecting a victim at random and beating them. Furthermore, prison camp managers are often SSD officials who failed[14] in some way, and are sent to run a *gwalliso* as punishment; this introduces a culture of bitterness and "taking it out on someone" from the top down.

Exile

Despite the fact that *gwalliso* inmates spend most of their waking life working in prison mines, factories, and farms—in return for below-subsistence rations and terrible living conditions—the DPRK apparently considers the system a costly one to maintain. Consequently, an old Korean method of dealing

---

14. For instance, an SSD agent who performed badly in an overseas mission to monitor the business activities of North Korean diplomats. An international posting such as this would be considered a very attractive one, as it involves travel and money-making opportunities. Being brought home from that posting to run a prison camp—with the implication that they would never be awarded a "decent" job again—would lead to bitterness.

with one's enemies is making a comeback. Though the DPRK has long exiled political "criminals" to the remote countryside, such a punishment is growing in frequency today.

The system is a very simple one. Enemies of the state are taken up to the mountains and left there with nothing. It is expected that they will die there. Though the authors know of no evidence relating to this, it is presumably the case that those who make their way down into a town or village can be punished severely if caught, since they do not possess the permit to be there. North Korea also has a number of uninhabited islands, and it is said that one can be punished by being exiled to one.

Sometimes, high-ranking officials find themselves surplus to requirements, and are given the "golden cage" treatment. Ri Yong Ho, once a very powerful military figure who ran the Pyongyang Defense Command, was pushed aside following the succession of Kim Jong Un. State media announced his retirement due to ill health, and praised him as a great servant of the country. He was given a luxurious home in the countryside—but one that he is not allowed to leave. In being away from his old network and the center of power in Pyongyang, his influence is now diminished. Whilst still maintaining the valuable pretense of Ri as a national hero by retiring rather than being seen to punish him, the regime is able to neutralize his power by keeping him under house arrest.

Chapter 5

Clothes, Fashion, and Trends

"Let's trim our hair in accordance with the socialist lifestyle," exhorted a now much-ridiculed (internationally at least) five-part television series first broadcast on Korean Central Television in 2004. The show made spurious arguments as to why long hair reduced intellectual performance, and named and shamed men who dared let their locks grow past their ears. Similarly, those who dress in any way unconventionally in North Korea have long been subject to punishment or public shaming. Jeans, for instance—which signify Americanism more than any other type of clothing—are banned. Wearers can even be sent to *rodong danryondae* (labor camps).

For both men and women, there are officially sanctioned hairstyles from which one should choose. Clothing should also be conservative—women who defect often express shock at the bright colors and revealing clothes worn by women in China and South Korea. However, as with media consumption and attitudes to capitalism, there are many today who have very little interest in looking as though they follow the socialist lifestyle. There are interesting trends developing in clothing, hair, cosmetics, beauty standards, and cosmetic surgery in

North Korea. Those who consider such things trivial should think again: these trends are changing how some people feel about the DPRK authorities, and even inspiring a few to defect.

Sartorial Crimes and the Fashion Police

But first, how would the DPRK government like its citizens to look? There are a few prescribed styles of clothing in North Korea. Many men, especially those aspiring toward an official position of some sort, wear "Mao suits," known locally as *yangbok*. In Korean, *yangbok* literally means "Western clothing," and usually refers to a suit. In the North, what is considered "Western" has a distinctly more Soviet implication, hence the high-collared, buttoned-up dark gray, black, or blue suits popularized by Stalin, and the variations worn by Chairman Mao and Kim Il Sung. The full set, jacket and trousers, sells for about US$20 in official markets, and probably much less in a *jangmadang*.

The suits are normally well-tailored, and cut from Chinese cloth originally intended for another purpose—it is not uncommon to buy what looks like Kim Jong Un's jacket only to find the inside is lined with fake Chinese Prada or Louis Vuitton logos. Like the more usual "Western" suit worn by businessmen elsewhere, North Korean *yangbok* comes with its own set of sartorial etiquette that the wearer is supposed to follow. White attachments similar to dog collars are sold separately, and are designed to be worn inside the outer collar so that a few milimeters of white material shows around the neck. To more conservative members of society, those who fail to observe this are committing a social sin.

Even for those who do not wear *yangbok*, there is an imperative to dress in a conservative, inconspicuous fashion. This isn't merely a matter of communist uniformity. *Monan doli jeong majneunda* ("the pointed stone meets with the chisel") is an expression that sums up traditional Korean attitudes to non-conformity, both north and south of the DMZ. While South Korea today is changing rapidly, and one can see brightly-colored clothing everywhere, it is the rare South Korean who truly rocks the boat in terms of fashion or life in general. Many young South Koreans today complain about the entrenched conformism of Korean society.[1] In having deliberately insulated North Koreans from alternatives and having punished ostentatious fashion (unlike the South in the post-dictatorship era), the DPRK authorities have merely added to this historic conformist orientation.

In practical terms, this means a lot of blue and black clothing. And for women, it certainly means dressing in an un-sexy manner. Traditional Korean *hanbok*, which hides rather than accentuates femininity, wins high approval from the DPRK authorities for its modesty and Korean-ness; women are expected to wear *hanbok* on national holidays and other special occasions. Short skirts, by contrast, are frowned upon, along with high heels, low cut dresses, and any kind of tight clothing. In fact, bright or sexy attire can even be interpreted as a form of dissent by the government. Even humble stud earrings were forbidden until 2010, according to defector accounts. Enforced by the Ministry of People's Security and zealous young students from the Kim Il Sung Socialist Youth League, a very real form of fashion police exists in North Korea, one that seeks to make sure its citizens are not dissenting in their dress or committing sartorial crimes.

---

1. For an example of this, see a satirical internet cartoon named "*jeongdap sahoi*" ("correct answer society"), which mocks the perceived need to enter the "right" university, get one of the few jobs considered "good," wear the same fashionable clothes that everyone else wears, and so on.

This fashion police concerns itself with hair, as well. Men with any kind of "long" hair (even to the extent where it covers their ears) can be punished. If their "crime" is particularly bad, they can be sent to labor camps; lesser transgressors may be subjected to self-criticism sessions, or at least forced to get a trim.[2] There are a much wider range of accepted styles for women; perming and braiding are both common. Dyeing, though, would be unacceptable. Some get away with dyeing their hair brown and claiming it's their natural color, but anything obviously dyed can result in a *rodong danryondae* sentence of a few months.

Brave New World

These days, there are many who break the rules. As with much social change in North Korea, the mid-1990s famine can be considered a turning point. The collapse of the Public Distribution System made people more independent, and more ready to ignore the government's rules. One source states that her hometown became "diverse" in terms of clothing styles in 1998. And furthermore, the currency redenomination of 2009 has reinforced this change, as it alienated the public even further from the rules and regulations of the state.

The death of Kim Jong Il in December 2011 has also had a significant impact. Kim's green *jamba* suit, which became an integral part of his image (and the subject of much international ridicule), had been popular, especially among men who wanted to give the impression of being powerful. Today, however, it is

---

2. During the Park Chung-hee era, South Korea also had fashion police who went around cutting men's hair. They even carried rulers to measure skirt length.

considered old fashioned. Successor Kim Jong Un's style of dress is also considered unfashionable, but he has other reasons for wearing a *yangbok*[3]: it reminds people of his grandfather.

Kim Jong Un's wife, Ri Sol Ju, is a trend-setter of sorts. Her style is typical of the new, rich Pyongyang woman, though not to an excessively showy extent. Interestingly, she sometimes wears brooches in place of the Kim Il Sung badges that are standard at official events. She also wears trouser suits and even high heels, which until recently carried an image of wantonness, but now signify femininity. Since Ms. Ri is both first lady and reasonably popular with North Koreans, she is setting a new example to young women in how to dress. The Moranbong Band, too, can be seen in a similar light; that a group supposedly created by Kim Jong Un himself can wear short skirts is effectively a green light to dress less conservatively.

So while the rules forbid bright colors, jeans, the dyeing of hair, and short skirts, it looks as though the Supreme Leader himself does not mind too much. And while the Socialist Youth League may still care, they do not care to the extent that connections or bribes cannot change their minds. One woman in her twenties, who left her hometown of Hoeryong (near the Chinese border) in October 2008, states that she was once caught wearing black jeans on the street by Youth League members. They took her away and harangued her for nine long hours, but then released her after her mother showed up. Her mother knew many senior officials, so the matter was dropped. Many will say that a payment in foreign currency should also have a similar effect.

---

3. Though Kim Jong Un's *yangbok* is woven from matte black pinstripes, and apparently cut from very expensive cloth imported from London's Savile Row.

There are, of course, those who are unable to pull rank or bribe their way out of trouble. In such cases, the fashion rule-breaker may be sent to a labor camp, for a period ranging from one or two months to a whole year. It should therefore come as no surprise that a disproportionate number of bolder dressers come from wealthy or elite families. North Korean society is above all governed by cash and connections.

Not all of the impetus for rule-breaking comes from within. In the era of the USB stick and the DVD, many North Koreans have seen South Korean fashion and have come to the conclusion that it is much better than their own. Much of this is celebrity-driven. For instance, faked versions of a pair of shoes worn by South Korean actress Kim Tae-hee went on sale in a Pyongyang department store for US$120. Kim Tae-hee is known to North Korean *hallyu* aficionados as the leading representative of South Korean beauty, and so those with the money will spend whatever it takes to copy her style. South Korean actor Won Bin is also popular in North Korea, so male fashion victims pay close attention to his hair and the clothes he wears.

Chongjin, Fashion Capital

The city of Chongjin, whose famine-era tragedy was so evocatively rendered in Barbara Demick's *Nothing to Envy*, is today developing a rather different reputation. Chongjin is a large industrial city far away from the strong ideological influence of Pyongyang. It is still under the firm grip of the state, but among many North Koreans, Chongjin is now a city of fashion. The average person there is still poor, but in the emerging capitalist era, this port city is growing in importance as a trading hub. Chongjin has thus become the first place where foreign fashions arrive.

Even Pyongyang cannot match Chongjin in terms of style. This may seem surprising, since Pyongyang is the seat of both new money and old power. But security is much stricter in the capital, with conformity more rigorously enforced. This means that clothes a young Pyongyang woman can only wear at home may be acceptable to wear in the street elsewhere.[4] Pyongyang is supposed to be the city of regime loyalists; Kim Jong Il is understood to have once said that his government could survive as long as he retained a firm grip on Pyongyang. He was much less interested in the provinces—and this is reflected both in the distribution of favors and the enforcement of laws.

Thus, Pyongyang is the only part of the country where the state is in full control of public order.[5] The government will still crack down hard on serious dissent wherever it arises, but generally, it lacks the resources and respect to compel people in the provinces to adhere to the full range of its rules and regulations. Chongjin administrators in particular are understood to have a looser approach to public order. Furthermore, Chongjin is both a border region city and a trading port. The combination of these factors makes Chongjin the closest North Korea has to a "Wild West."

---

4. One will also see women riding bicycles in every city and town of North Korea, except Pyongyang. Kim Jong Il once banned the practice, but the rule was only enforced in the capital. The ban was later lifted, but the aversion remains.

5. Nearby Pyongsong, a bumpy one-hour drive from Pyongyang, is a heartland of the new North Korean grassroots capitalism. It is close enough to the capital to house a middle class, but far away enough to be just beyond the reach of absolute control. It is here, some analysts argue, that some kind of "middle class uprising" against the government may begin, if an uprising is ever a remote possibility. Pyongsong residents do have special reason to be angry these days: their city was once officially part of greater Pyongyang, but now, it is not. Their days of relative generosity from the state thus came to an end.

Chongjin traders frequently receive 100 kilogram packages of clothes by boat from Japan. Again, the authorities frown on this—but not to the extent that local Chongjin officials cannot be paid to look the other way. The contents of such packages will be unknown until opened, and as a precaution, all the labels that identify each item's country of origin are removed. And though the random jackets, jeans, skirts, and other items they contain are cast-offs that Japanese consumers no longer want, they are of a much higher quality and more fashionable than anything made in North Korea (or China, for that matter).

For the young women of Chongjin, then, even Ri Sol Ju's style is not particularly impressive. One young female defector from the city states that Ms. Ri's red-and-black check outfit was "nothing special," although she did praise a green dress the first lady famously wore when out in public with Kim Jong Un. She also claims that Ms. Ri's hairstyle is "*jom chonseuropda*" (roughly translated, "a bit dowdy"), and the she never wears anything that other North Korean women could not get away with. Some Pyongyang sources, though, call Ms. Ri a rule-breaker—thus highlighting the differences between the two cities.

North Korea has its own specially developed fabric, named vinylon, which government propaganda often mentions as an example of DPRK innovation. Unfortunately, vinylon is uncomfortable, not to mention un-cool. To young North Koreans, virtually anything made in North Korea is undesirable. And though Japan ranks alongside the United States as a chief enemy state, its products are sought-after. When the 100 kilogram packages are opened, then, people want to keep many of the items for themselves and their friends. So while Japanese clothes brought in through Chongjin do end up all over the country, locals get the first pick.

What are Chongjin people wearing today? For those who are interested in such trends, Chongjin is known as the place in North Korea where skinny jeans first became popular. One defector, who left in 2010, states that both jeans and any type of clothing that shows off the body were forbidden—but that she and many others were wearing flared skinny jeans that "make your legs look slim and good so you can show off."[6] For young women, showing off in this way seems to be a new and liberating experience.

Even in Chongjin though, blue jeans are beyond the pale. Young people watch foreign movies and see their favorite actors and actresses wearing them, but since "they just look too foreign," Youth League officials are more likely to take exception. People therefore tend to wear less conspicuous black jeans, flared or otherwise. To wear black jeans in North Korea, one should also wear a long coat, to make it more difficult for a police officer to notice them. It is also wiser to wear jeans after nightfall, though there are those who are brave enough to take the risk in broad daylight. Under cover of darkness, there are other fashions that make an appearance, too. Short skirts worn with black stockings are popular in Chongjin and other cities, particularly with young women going to meet their boyfriends in the evening.

6. The flared lower part also means that, from a quick glance, one cannot readily notice that the jeans are also of the skinny variety—especially if the wearer also has a long coat on.

Local Knock-offs

Not all of the fashionable clothing in North Korea is imported. Plenty is made at home, by tailors and cobblers who respond to the demands of the market. Most of what they produce is cheap, but there are a few highly-skilled artisans who can, for instance, make virtually identical copies of Burberry's famed trenchcoats. These eventually sell to members of the new financial elite for around US$300.

South Koreans are fond of saying that although China produces the world's greatest volume of designer fakes, nobody beats local copycats on quality. Thus, Chinese tourists in Seoul's Myeongdong district love loading up on knock-off Louis Vuitton bags, Gucci belts, and any number of other fake items. North Korea is rather similar: Chinese merchants reportedly express surprise at the superior quality of copy items produced in the Kangsun area of Nampho, a city which lies at the mouth of the Taedonggang river, downstream from Pyongyang.

Kangsun is North Korea's knock-off capital, turning out US$10 tailored dress shirts modeled on famous brands, and trousers that may cost a few dollars more than that. Tailors there obtain items of clothing from China and Japan, and work out how to copy them. Their end products are popular with wealthy young people—students at elite institutions like Kim Il Sung University, for example.

Apparently, some Kangsun tailors make copies of clothes worn by Ri Sol Ju, based on the demands of wealthy Pyongyang women. But the overall story is one of *hallyu* internationalism: they take Chinese cloth, and use it to copy the designer outfits of South Korean celebrities, and even lingerie seen in South Korean and American movies. If a Southern drama series or movie becomes an underground hit in North Korea—via USB or DVD—tailors will work out how to fake the clothes worn by its stars. Those who can do this quickly make a decent living.

It would fly in the face of conventional opinion to suggest that North Koreans consider South Koreans cool and worthy of emulating. But thanks to their familiarity with South Korean TV and movies via USB sticks and DVDs, North Koreans now see Southerners as tall, good-looking people with a much better standard of living than them. Some talking heads argue that North Korea can never pursue economic reform because any openness would enable North Koreans to "find out" about the superior quality of life that exists south of the DMZ. But the truth is this: North Koreans already know about it. That is not to say that they want to overthrow the regime—this is still something that would not occur to most North Koreans—but that they want the regime to pursue economic reform and openness, so that all the people can enjoy a better quality of life.

Beauty Products and Treatments

North Koreans are fond of saying that one can buy anything in a *jangmadang* other than a cat's horn. This exotic-sounding expression merely means that the only things that cannot be bought there are things that do not exist. As noted, cans of Coca-Cola, DVDs of South Korean and American movies, and home-brewed alcohol are all available. Women's make-up is also popular. For wealthier women shopping at Pyongyang markets, this means eye shadow, mascara, and everything else that a modern woman would want to beautify herself with. For middle-income women, one particular product is considered good enough to get the job done: BB cream.

BB ("blemish balm") cream was invented in Germany, but popularized in South Korea. South Korean women have been using it since the 1980s to cover blemishes and give the skin a smooth, consistent appearance. It has since caught on around the world as a kind of "miracle" product that can produce an effect almost as good as proper make-up, at a fraction of the expense and effort. For the hard-working urban North Korean woman with a small amount of disposable income, BB cream is therefore a godsend. It is replacing the inferior homemade concoctions of hair oil and powder that beauty-conscious North Korean women used to favor.

As with most other *jangmadang* products, BB cream is imported from China. Some creams are made in China as well, but the most desirable ones are made in South Korea, and are popular in spite of their higher cost. BB cream is now a standard household item in Pyongyang, and is becoming so in other cities. However, as may be expected, few in the countryside use it. For the average rural woman, life still centers on farming, and the preparation of food for the family table—much as it does in poor countries the world over.

Other than BB cream, South Korea is especially famous for one rather more extreme form of beauty treatment. High-quality, competitively-priced plastic surgery is one of the South's twenty-first century growth industries, drawing in both domestic and foreign customers. Women from China, Japan, and further afield, travel to Seoul in their droves to have painful jawline reconstructions, breast enlargements, liposuction, double-eyelid procedures, and botox injections. Plastic surgery is now an utterly normal thing among young South Korean women. The trend is driven not by vanity, but rather, competition. South Korea is possibly the most intensely competitive society in the world—people there compete over academic achievement, jobs, status symbols, and physical appearance, to a much greater extent than the average Westerner would imagine possible. South Korean competitiveness surprises North Korean defectors, too, when they arrive. But having said that, the plastic surgery craze is also now spreading northwards.

As with fashion, the driving force is South Korean television and movies. South Korean actors and actresses are considered physically very attractive—and a large part of the reason for that is the plastic surgery and botox treatments that most of them have. However, because of a lack of money and a shortage of doctors who know how to perform such operations, there is but one truly common procedure—the double-eyelid operation.

There is a common belief in East Asia that big eyes, with fold lines along the lids, are attractive. Some people are naturally born with them, but most are not. This is easily "corrected" with a simple surgical procedure called blepharoplasty, which requires very little in the way of medical skill, and can be completed in under ten minutes.[7] In North Korea, the wealthy can have it done properly, by paying a real surgeon. For most, though, the operation is done in a very "back street" fashion. In such cases the procedure costs as little as US$2, and is performed in the patient's home—without the aid of anesthetic. Many of those who perform the operation are not even doctors. It is in fact possible for anyone to learn how to make an eyelid fold, and start offering the service. Those who do it well will benefit from word of mouth, and be able to make a good living.

---

7. There are even step-by-step videos on YouTube that show you how to do it yourself!

As with all forms of plastic surgery, the double-eyelid procedure is illegal in North Korea. It is, however, so common among young urban women of all social classes that the authorities cannot do very much about it. Proving someone has undergone the operation is also difficult, since there are some who were born with double eyelids. Those caught may also be able to get friends and relatives to state that their double eyelids are natural. And even when guilt is established, this is nothing that a bribe cannot fix.

There are also many women who have their eyebrows tattooed, or even their lips. Such work costs even less than eyelid surgery. And now, there are a very small number of women—mostly in Pyongyang, and from the very wealthy classes—who are having nose jobs. This is believed to be particularly popular among young women with ambitions in acting or music. But South Korea's "aesthetic surgery" trend started among the wealthy elite, and considering that the North Korean economy is undergoing serious real bottom-up change, it looks very likely that both options and the availability of plastic surgery in North Korea will increase in the coming years.

From the Unnatural to the Most Natural

International media representation of North Koreans tends to strip them of agency. The DPRK citizen is shown as either a blind follower of state propaganda, or a helpless victim of it. But the fact that there are young North Koreans who are prepared to risk severe punishment—as well as the strong disapproval of elders[8]—simply to look good, should disabuse the

---

8. Those who dye their hair, for instance, are not just rule-breakers—they are also seen as "crazy" by older North Koreans, according to one defec-

reader of such a simplified, caricaturish notion.

Those who adhere to the stereotypical view should consider the case of the growing "rooms by the hour" cottage industry that exists in all North Korean cities. As with people the world over, North Koreans have desires, and no amount of prohibition or social disgrace is going to stop those desires from being expressed in the end. In a country where pre-marital sex is frowned upon, and even holding hands in public can result in harsh words from Youth League goons, there are young people who engage in the risky business of renting private apartments merely for the length of time it takes to have sex. Young South Korean couples have the option of "love motels," which form a huge industry there. But North Koreans have no such choice—and this has resulted in a grassroots, free-market solution.

In any given big city neighborhood, there will be an *ajumma*—a middle-aged lady—known to let out her apartment by the hour. Her preferred time will be in the afternoon, when her children are at school, and her husband is at work. An amorous couple will knock on her door, and hand over some cash. The *ajumma* then leaves them alone, perhaps for an hour or two. She may take a walk in a local park, or spend the money she received on goods at the nearest *jangmadang*. The process is very simple, but it acts as a reasonable summary of the people's adaptation to post-famine North Korea: it is illegal; it is informal; it corresponds to basic human needs; and, it is one hundred percent capitalist.

tor. As Korean culture has a strong tradition of age-based hierarchy, this is no small matter.

Chapter 6

Communications

One of the most noticeable changes to have taken place in North Korea in the past five years is the rise of the cell phone. Since the 2008 launch of network operator Koryolink, more than two and a half million North Koreans have bought cellular phones and registered with the service. Much as it was in the early 1990s in the developed world, the mobile is seen as both a status symbol and an invaluable tool for business.

As in many poor countries, North Koreans are skipping the mass adoption of landlines, and proceeding straight into mobile telephony. It is, in fact, a rare private home that contains its own landline. It was not until 1997 that the DPRK replaced its army of button-pressers with automated telephone exchange technology. But while the authorities are generally resistant to change, Koryolink is both easily monitored and a good source of hard currency for the state. There is another, more exciting, side to the North Korean mobile revolution, though: there are also those who connect to Chinese mobile networks, gaining the power to communicate and conduct business deals away from the prying eyes of the state.

A Short History of the Cell Phone in North Korea

The first two mobile networks in North Korea were short-lived. Hong Kong firm Lancelot Holdings set up a small network in Pyongyang and Nampho in 1998, and in 2002 Thai firm Loxley Pacific built Sunnet, a network which one year later had managed to amass just 20,000 subscribers. This was due to the fact that it was restricted to elites; apparently, one had to at least be a vice-chairman of a Provincial People's Committee to have one. The service was geographically restricted, too, in only being available in the Rajin-Sonbong free economic zone, Kumgang mountain resort, and Pyongyang.

However, on May 24, 2004, cell phones were suddenly banned by the government. The rumor was that the massive explosion at Ryongchon that April 22 had been a deliberate bombing, with the detonation triggered by cell phone. Kim Jong Il had passed through the station just hours before, naturally giving weight to the theory that an attempted assassination had taken place. Nearly 2,000 nearby homes were destroyed by the blast, and the government even took the rare step of appealing for outside help in coping with the disaster. For many Korea-watchers, the timing of the ban was confirmation enough of the link between mobile technology and the Ryongchon explosion. However, as with all unconfirmed stories about North Korea, it is important to leave plenty of room in one's mind for doubt.

Regardless, it was to be another four-and-a-half years before Kim Jong Il allowed another cellular phone network in North Korea. In December 2008, Egyptian firm Orascom Telecom began operating Koryolink as a joint venture between itself and the DPRK, with the former holding 75 percent of shares. This time, the results were more successful: from an initial subscriber base of less than 10,000, user numbers climbed dramatically, reaching 432,000 in December 2010 (the second anniversary of opening), one million in February 2012, and two million in late May 2013.

A majority of Orascom Telecom's shares were acquired by Russian telecoms firm Vimpelcom in 2010. Koryolink was not part of the deal, though—along with Orascom Telecom's Egyptian and Lebanese interests, Koryolink was reconstituted as part of a new firm, OTMT. This rump company has its primary listing on the Cairo Stock Exchange. Those tempted by extreme frontier markets investing—as well as those curious about the extent of genuine restrictions on North Korean business in the sanctions era—may be interested to know that OTMT also has a secondary listing on the London Stock Exchange. The DPRK owns a 25 percent interest in Koryolink, so those who buy OTMT shares (from London or Cairo) become business partners with Kim Jong Un.

Using Your Koryolink Phone

These days, one can see Koryolink billboard adverts in Pyongyang, and images of people using mobiles in state media. The network itself extends to all towns and cities, as well as highways and railway lines. In having two and a half million subscribers, the service is no longer the preserve of the traditional elite; it is now accessible to the rising merchant class as well. International calls and internet access are still blocked—and probably will remain so for a very long time—but it is at least now a normal sight to see North Koreans making phone calls and sending text messages. A majority of Pyongyangites between 20 and 50 years of age have cell phones. Some even have smartphones, though the lack of internet access limits their value. If one wants to download an app in North Korea, one has to go to a Koryolink shop and pay for a member of the staff to physically install it on one's smartphone.

But how does one go about buying and registering a cell phone in North Korea? As with everything else in today's DPRK, the only real requirement is money. Two hundred US dollars gets you a handset and registration at a Koryolink shop. This is payable in foreign currency, not North Korean won. It is worth noting that this is yet another example of the state's complicity in, and acceptance of, marketization.

There is no contract billing system for call minutes, other than a basic 3,000 North Korean won per month charge. The only option for extra is pay-as-you-go, so when one's monthly allotted 200 minutes (and 20 text messages) run out, one must go back to the shop and purchase additional credit. This is also done with foreign currency—as of early 2013, US$8.40 gave the user 200 additional minutes.

In such a poor country, these costs—particularly the US$200 set-up cost—are prohibitively expensive for most people outside of Pyongyang. But the fact that over ten percent of the population has signed up is instructive. Thanks to post-famine marketization, there are now many people who can afford it. In fact, those who trade in North Korea are coming to see phones as not just a luxury, but rather a necessary business expense. In the past, information about prices in other regions of the country was hard to come by. The same was true regarding information about potential suppliers and customers. But now, it simply takes a quick phone call or text message to find out. Interestingly, this is having a leveling effect on the prices of goods at markets around the country. The cell phone is reducing cross-market arbitrage opportunities, making trading less profitable (but prices more reasonable for end consumers).[1] The biggest loser in this process is, naturally, the trader who does not possess a phone.

For the trading *ajumma,* then, the phone is an important business tool. But for young people, it is probably more of a status symbol—something to pressure your parents into buying for you, so you can appear wealthy and cosmopolitan.[2] For this reason, there are North Koreans who possess phones that they cannot afford to use.[3] One source states that for many, the cell phone is an "expensive torch"—in other words, a showy item whose only practical use comes from its backlight. In a country where power cuts are extremely common, this is perhaps to be expected. (It is reportedly much more fashionable to whip out one's phone during a blackout than a torch.)

In North Korea, your number also says something about your status. While ordinary people have numbers beginning with 191 or 193 (followed by seven other digits), an elite "special registrant" will have a number beginning with 195. There are around 300,000 such special registrants, most of whom are party members, military officers, and government officials. These 195 numbers operate on a completely separate network to Koryolink. The network was installed by Orascom as a con-

---

1. This also has the effect of increasing market efficiency, however, and increases competition between traders.
2. Several sources claim that young men use phones to impress women. Those with the money will now want to show off with a smartphone, despite the fact that one cannot connect to the internet in North Korea. The DPRK even has its own smartphone now, the Arirang. Much like the Samjiyon tablet, though, it is almost certainly not DPRK-made, and regardless, those with the money will buy a foreign brand. The Arirang is best seen as a would-be symbol of national pride and/or intent.
3. There are even dummy cell phones for sale at *jangmadang.* Children also enjoy playing with toy cell phones.

dition of being allowed to operate in the country, but unlike Koryolink, it is 100 percent owned by the DPRK. The lucky few who use it receive an extra 100 minutes of talk time and ten extra text messages per month. They may also top up for 840 North Korean won, a sum worth around ten US cents on the open market at the time of writing. Clearly this is not a benefit either the state or Orascom will ever want to extend to the average citizen.

On the Border

Though Koryolink empowers individuals in terms of the business they can conduct, and brings them the lifestyle convenience that first amazed the rich world in the 1980s, one should not jump to the conclusion that the network has any power to undermine state control. Koryolink is heavily monitored—text messages are monitored in real-time, for instance—and for that reason it may even help maintain control.

It is also, of course, a reliable and growing source of income for the state. OTMT has never released data on Koryolink other than subscriber numbers, but before the corporate reorganization, gross profit margins were around 80 percent on an average revenue per user of almost US$15 per quarter. With a user base of over two million ordinary registrants, the share of profit accruing to the state will be in the low tens of millions per year. Added to that are the huge margins earned on handsets, which are marked up by two or three times their real value.[4] According to accountants Deloitte, Koryolink has built

---

4. Handsets are paid for in foreign currency—so the government, in being unable to control the use of foreign currency, is essentially admitting, if you can't beat them, join them (and make money from them).

up US$422 million of cash (presumably from core business operations) in North Korea. How much of this OTMT will ever be able to take out of North Korea, though, is a question of great concern to the OTMT management. So far, the answer has been "zero."

So far, so good for the regime, then. But not all mobile telephony is officially welcomed. Over the past 15 years, phones that access Chinese mobile networks in border cities like Sinuiju, Hyesan, and Hoeryeong have helped change the fortunes of those living near the superpower to the north. Chinese phones are being used to talk to family members living in China and South Korea, and also to arrange trade, pass information back and forth, and even facilitate defections.

For such reasons, it is highly illegal in North Korea to connect to a Chinese mobile network. During occasional clampdowns, punishments can be extremely severe—execution is not unknown. But the authorities can never hope to eradicate the practice, due to the existence of financial incentives. Chinese traders bringing phones through in bulk simply cut officials in on the deal, and those who are caught using Chinese phones can escape punishment most of the time by simply paying a bribe.

Officials are even directly involved in the business. One defector source who lived near the Chinese border states that he was caught using a Chinese phone by an MPS officer, and was forced to pay a bribe of 3000 yuan to get away. His phone was confiscated as well, but since he could not conduct his cross-border business without one, he later went back to the very same official and bought the handset back from him for 1800 yuan. As a precaution against being caught again, he later purchased another one from the same MPS officer as a back-up, at a slightly lower price.

Further undermining state control, in a psychological sense at least, is the increased use of South Korean-made phones among Chinese network users. There are multiple reasons for this, but the most important are: South Korean products are fashionable, due to the *hallyu* effect; they tend to be of higher quality, and are believed to get better reception; and, they always offer Korean language menus. The wealthy, and those who need high call quality for their business needs, are increasingly carrying LG or Samsung handsets.

There is also money to be made in charging people to use one's China-linked mobile. Over half of those who have made calls out of North Korea with Chinese phones do not actually possess one themselves. The vast majority of phone owners do allow others to make calls for a fee, and will also let friends and family use them for free. The fact that people are now confident enough to let others use their illegal phones offers clear evidence that North Koreans in border regions now have much less fear of authority, and are also less concerned about the possibility of being informed upon. Before the famine, even family members would sometimes inform on each other, either out of fear or the belief that it was the "right" thing to do. This is certainly no longer the case.[5]

That said, people do take precautions when making calls. To prevent signal tracing, phone owners keep their handsets switched off until they actually need to use them. For the same reason, call length is kept short—a duration of over five minutes would be considered excessive. Some use secret, pre-ar-

---

5. This is an important development. Such was the strength of state control that in the past, many children considered it morally correct to inform on their parents. The breaking of the social contract due to the famine, and the post-famine growth of cynicism toward the regime, is largely responsible for this welcome change.

ranged code words when discussing particularly sensitive topics, such as defections.

Some take caution to unusual levels. One defector (who left North Korea in November 2010) talks of filling a sink with water and placing a rice-cooker lid on his head every time he made a call on an illicit Chinese phone. Apparently, there was a belief that this would stop mobile signals from being traced. This shows that despite recent changes, North Korea is still a very closed society—in the absence of proper information, all manner of bizarre ideas and conspiracy theories are able to spread.

Jamming and External Radio Broadcasting

The state cannot afford to comprehensively jam foreign signals, as it requires constant transmission at high power. Nevertheless, DPRK authorities are increasingly attempting to frustrate users of Chinese mobile networks. Jamming results in broken calls, and forces users to head up into the hills for better reception—where signal detectors have also been set up, to trace and catch people. Particularly in the era of Kim Jong Un, in which the state seeks to tighten border security and prevent defections, jamming is a growing source of frustration for those in the border regions. But North Koreans have been using Chinese phones for well over a decade now, and are not going to give up on their main link to the outside world. And, of course, a phone user who gets caught will merely have to pay a bribe, unless there is a crackdown or they are apprehended by a particularly zealous policeman.

Radio transmissions from outside North Korea are also subject to jamming attempts, although again, those who want to listen to them will still be able to find a way to listen. The area around the demilitarized zone (DMZ) is one of the heaviest for radio traffic in the world. Perhaps the most interesting—and least talked about—case of external broadcasting into the North is South Korea's "numbers station," a regular broadcast which has existed for decades, despite the DPRK's attempts to block it.

Numbers stations transmit coded messages for the benefit of secret agents. It is well-known that there are North Korean agents in South Korea. But the reverse is also true, and one of the main ways South Korea[6] communicates with its agents is by sending a stream of numbers read out by an announcer, over a variety of AM frequencies. Some broadcasts begin with the North Korean song *Bangapseumnida* ("Nice to Meet You"), although it is not unusual to now hear Beethoven's 8th Piano Sonata introduce a broadcast. When the song is over, a female voice begins reading out numbers: "Fifty-six. Thirty-one. Seventy-three," and so on, using the military style of reading numbers in Korean that avoids ambiguity. For the ordinary listener, this sounds like nothing more than a suspicious bingo game. But for the agent with his/her codebook, those numbers contain instructions.

North Korea once had a numbers station of its own (and North Korean spies were found with codebooks in South Korea in the 1990s), but it is generally believed that it was discontinued around the year 2000.[7] This is not evidence of diminished North Korean interest in espionage, though. The

---

6. Of course, nobody publicly claims ownership of a numbers station. But one can assume with a reasonable degree of certainty that this particular numbers station is South Korean.

7. Amateur radio enthusiasts who had monitored the North Korean station for years last reported hearing a broadcast in 2000. The South Korean station, known as "V24" to its listeners, still broadcasts.

South is a much more open country, and it is therefore eminently possible for Northern agents stationed there to receive instructions via phone, mail, or the internet.

Both North and South are involved in propaganda broadcasting as well. Both sides target each other with news broadcasts over short and medium wave, and both defend themselves through jamming—though again, with limited degrees of success. The DPRK's attempt at propaganda radio is called *Choson-ui Sori* (Voice of Korea), and broadcasts in Korean, English, Japanese, Chinese, French, German, Russian, Spanish, and Arabic. Voice of Korea plays music and broadcasts news with a heavy bias against South Korea's "lackey" leaders and the "imperialist" United States. Seoul attempts to jam this with a repetitive chugging sound, played on the same frequency, but it is generally possible to receive a clear enough signal on high ground anywhere in South Korea.[8] The same is sometimes true of North Korea's main radio station, *Choson Joongang Bangsong* (Korea Central Broadcasting).

The South has an equivalent to Voice of Korea, *Heuimangeui Meari* (Echo of Hope), as well as KBS's *Hanminjok Bangsong* (Korean Ethnic Broadcasting), which targets ethnic Koreans living outside of South Korea (rather than merely just North Koreans). The DPRK attempts to block these stations, as well as other KBS radio broadcasts, with a sound similar to that of a jet plane taking off.

There are also US government-funded efforts to target North Korean radio listeners, such as Voice of America and Radio Free Asia's Korean language broadcasts. Additionally,

---

8. But be warned, doing so is actually against South Korea's National Security Law.

and more importantly, there are independent[9] broadcasters such as Open Radio for North Korea, Radio Free Chosun, North Korea Reform Radio, and Free North Korea Radio, which operate from the South and are often at least partly staffed by defectors. There are also similar Japanese organizations targeting North Korean listeners, and at least two Christian stations doing the same.[10]

The Impact of Radio

As with televisions, radios legally sold in North Korea come only with access to preset DPRK channels. Possession of either a modified radio or a foreign radio with across-the-band tuning is punishable by law. But as may be expected, this does not stop *jangmadang* traders and Chinese merchants from selling them. And being caught with one is something a bribe can usually fix. A typical official sees a radio owner as a meal ticket, good for a few dollars and the radio set itself. The radio is confiscated, and re-sold—also to the benefit of the official. Prosecuting the owner would simply take away this profit opportunity. Illicit radio listening is therefore able to flourish, facilitated by radios brought in from China, and the illegal modification of North Korean radio sets.

That said, foreign radio is not as popular as foreign TV and movies in North Korea. The reason for this is actually very

9. Though some are partly funded by the National Endowment for Democracy, which is itself funded by the US government.
10. There is also a secret station based in western Seoul that broadcasts to the North and poses as an "underground pirate radio station." It plays old songs from the South, and news reports about the activities of the South Korean president. The South Korean government does not acknowledge its existence, and its location in a field of transmitter towers is censored from satellite imagery on South Korean mapping websites.

simple: just like people in the rest of the world, North Koreans tend to find TV more entertaining.[11] There is also an issue with reception: one does not need to be able to receive a reliable electronic signal to watch a DVD of the South Korean drama *Winter Sonata*. Thus, as of 2010, around half of defectors surveyed had watched foreign TV, whilst only 27 percent had listened to foreign radio. This is despite the fact that radios are much cheaper, can run on batteries as well as unreliable North Korean electricity, and have been commonly available since the famine in the mid-1990s.

Radio, though, does have great power. Although people find it less entertaining than TV, they also consider it the most trustworthy and informative medium. This is not just true of regular listeners, but also of North Koreans in general. This is because radio aimed at North Korea tends to be news-heavy, rather than full of drama series. And because much radio content is specifically intended for North Koreans, it deals with topics they care about, and fills an information gap left by the lack of genuine detail that pervades state media. For this reason, radio's relative lack of audience is compensated for by a word of mouth multiplier effect. Word about some particularly interesting news heard on the radio travels further and faster than talk about South Korean TV.

Radio is the only real-time source of North Korea-related information available to the average North Korean. The fact that one can hear about some future event on the radio—an incoming aid shipment, for example—and then witness it for oneself, confirms the trustworthiness of the medium. Often,

---

11. That said, the growth of foreign TV in North Korea has not caused existing radio listeners to switch off. Many consume both. Estimates suggest that radio listenership has stayed roughly constant since the growth of DVD/USB-led TV and movie consumption.

DPRK state media will simply not mention important events, or will delay reporting of them.

Radio from South Korea is considered more trustworthy than that beamed in from other countries. Why? Firstly, there is still a great deal of cultural overlap between North and South. And secondly, North Koreans have been told for years that, despite the South being ruled by a "puppet clique," South Koreans are still their brothers and sisters.[12] Voice of America is, on the other hand, produced by an alien enemy.[13] Although Hollywood movies on DVD and USB are now changing perceptions, North Koreans are still infinitely more likely to identify with South Koreans than with Americans.

Radio produced by defectors is especially powerful. To hear someone with a Northern accent criticizing Kim Jong Il and telling of their new life in Seoul—where life is not perfect, but at least materially much better than in the North—is both astonishing and inspiring. Broadcasts featuring defectors provide psychological support and hope to those thinking about trying to leave North Korea.

Who, When, and What

Foreign radio in North Korea seems to have a more clandestine aspect than foreign TV. This is due to its content, which is more North Korea-focused, transgressive, and potentially

---

12. Defectors arriving in South Korea are often disappointed when they find out that the reverse is not true. Few South Koreans these days take an active interest in reunification or North Korea in general, and even fewer try to help defectors.

13. The BBC has also considered extending its foreign-language services to include the Korean peninsula but has so far been stalled by widespread UK government funding cuts.

threatening to the regime. Those who listen to foreign radio tend to listen under cover of darkness, the most popular listening hours being 10 p.m. to 1 a.m. For that reason, all of the DPRK-focused external broadcasters operate at nighttime rather than daytime.

Most broadcasts are on shortwave frequencies. This is because shortwave signals can (unlike, say, standard FM public broadcast-range signals) bounce off the ionosphere, and travel long distances. Neither the DPRK nor China would allow North Korea-targeted independent broadcasting on their territory, but shortwave makes this an irrelevance. However, shortwave broadcasting does bring one additional complication: shortwave sets are not legally sold in North Korea. Chinese traders do bring them in, and technicians may also modify existing radios. But a substantial minority of radio owners still do not have access to shortwave. There are, therefore, increasing efforts by North Korea human rights campaigners to flood the country with shortwave receivers.

But there are still millions who listen. It is, in fact, possible to segment North Korean radio listeners by age, background, and social status, just as researchers do in other countries. Overall, men are more interested in radio than women, and the older are more interested than the young. It is understood that elites, especially the more worldly and well-educated, prefer hard news, particularly news relating to North–South relations. The more ambitious or successful of the new, emerging trading class have similar tastes, but often for commercial reasons. A big incoming rice shipment as part of an aid package would drive down the price of rice at the *jangmadang*. Increased UN sanctions would affect the price and availability of certain goods. A change in the level of Sino–DPRK border security would have a similar effect, and possibly affect the exchange rate as well. Crackdowns may make it dangerous to trade certain items. One would never hear such potentially lucrative information in a timely fashion from DPRK media, so foreign radio news is a must for the serious North Korean trader.

The less educated tend to prefer "lighter" broadcasts, such as those featuring letters from defectors to those back home. Though less "newsy," such content is also extremely powerful, as it still contains information about the differences between North and South, and is emotionally gripping. It can also make defection seem a less daunting matter. There are even those who have said that this kind of broadcast inspired them to defect.

Segmented targeting that reflects such differences is now becoming possible. Listeners have an increasingly wide variety of choices: the number of DPRK-focused stations is now in double figures. This has enabled listeners to become more discerning, switching off broadcasts they find uninteresting and seeking out something else. Surveys and discussions show that previously, radio owners would persist with a foreign broadcast, even if they found it dull, or could not get a good signal. These days, they move on, just as the rest of us do.

Chapter 7

Social Division

Just as the DPRK government has different factions with different agendas, the North Korean public is not the single-minded, robotic mass commonly portrayed by both North Korean state media and international media. At risk of stating the obvious, North Koreans can be as different from each other as South Koreans can.

In modern North Korea, three particular areas of social cleavage can tell us a great deal about the nature of the country: social class, ethnic origin, and regional background. The first two may seem surprising, as North Korea is commonly perceived as a communist (i.e., classless),[1] as well as ethnically homogeneous, country. North Korea, though, has a government-created system of social hierarchy, as well as a small but highly influential community of ethnic Chinese who are at the

---

1. The DPRK has in fact all but completely shunned the "communist" label, opting instead to focus on its own bastardization of Marxist philosophy and the Korean independence movement in the form of *Juche*, or self-reliance. Although portraits of Marx and Lenin were eventually removed from Kim Il Sung square in the 2010s, those brought up in former Soviet states granted the opportunity to wander Pyongyang's streets may feel as though they have stepped through a time machine.

vanguard of North Korea's growing informal trade and infor-mation exchange with the outside world.

The third is more obvious—the phenomenon of capital city dwellers looking down on country folk, for instance, is cer-tainly not confined to North Korea—but regional differences can also give us some idea as to where any major political or socio-economic change may occur in the future. Rural North Korea exists much as it always has, but a great many people in the northeast are now well informed of events in the outside world, and are also disappointed in the Kim regime. Pyong-yangites are also increasingly enlightened, but their interests are more closely aligned with the system, perhaps because many lead comparatively comfortable lives. For this reason, it is arguably the northeastern provinces of Ryanggang and North Hamgyong that we should be watching most closely.

Social Class

One may expect a socialist country to pursue a "classless soci-ety" as an eventual core goal. But North Korea is much closer to being a traditional Korean society than a socialist one. Up until the Gabo Reforms of 1894 (which officially ended Ko-rea's formal class distinctions), Korea had for centuries been a feudal society marked by strong class differences. And while the Japanese colonial period (1910–1945), the Korean War of 1950–53, and Kim Il Sung's land reforms[2] saw the obliteration of the old social order, Kim saw fit to construct a new class system, based on loyalty to his government.

---

2. There are plenty of people in South Korea who possess old deeds to land in North Korea. In the event of reunification, the question of how to deal with these numerous claims will become an important one.

The Workers' Party Politburo May 30th Resolution of 1957 introduced the concept of dividing North Korean society into loyal, neutral, and hostile groups. Broadly, loyalists were to be drawn from among those who fought alongside Kim Il Sung or from forces that pledged allegiance to him; socialist intellectuals and revolutionaries; and those who fought for the DPRK during the Korean War. Hostile persons were those who had been landowners and capitalists; those who had relatives and/or strong connections with South Korea; religious groups (including Christians and shamanists); and collaborators with the old Japanese colonial regime. Neutrals were those who fell between the two. A series of lengthy investigations into the colonial era and military activities of every North Korean's male relatives—the DPRK is patrilinealist, as well as being infected with a feudal mindset—was conducted.

This was the effective starting point of the *songbun* system of social classification that exists to this day, exerting an influence on each individual's destiny in the DPRK. The most common and long-standing figures state that 28 percent of North Koreans are in the loyal class, 45 percent in the neutral class, and 27 percent in the hostile class. It is far easier to have one's *songbun* downgraded than upgraded, though; one simple political mistake could bring one's whole family into a lower class. For that reason, the hostile group estimate may well be on the low side.[3]

Though *songbun* is now a highly entrenched system that covers the whole of North Korean society, it is not necessarily something that people are aware of on a day-to-day basis. The government does not tell citizens, "Mr. Kim, you are designated

---

3. Dr. Oh Kongdan of the Brookings Institution has stated that 40 percent may be more realistic.

as a hostile person, and will therefore never be given a good job." In fact, many people are not aware of their official *songbun* status. That some people are treated better than others merely on the basis of their lineage can even seem natural in the light of how Korean society had always functioned. That is not to say that people approve of it, of course.

Songbun, however, is a properly organized system. Your status appears on your government file, and whenever you request a promotion, apply to a university, or are arrested, for instance, the relevant decision-makers will take your *songbun* rating into account. And though virtually everything is for sale in today's North Korea (better *songbun* being a rare exception), *songbun* investigations are very thorough and involve many layers of bureaucracy: local police chiefs, residency registration officials, and section chiefs of the Ministry of People's Security all have to agree on a classification, and the higher up the social ladder one goes, the greater the involvement of the State Security Department as well. The number of people one would need to bribe to significantly alter one's *songbun* would render the whole venture impossible.

Bad *songbun* could have an effect on a person's life in a very diverse range of ways. One defector talks of failing to be selected for a national sports team due to her unfortunate background. The military does not allow those of the very lowest *songbun* to serve. Many speak of being passed over for jobs in favor of lesser-qualified, but better-born, competitors. Similarly, a person of good *songbun* who commits a crime may find leniency from a judge, where one with bad *songbun* would not. The best schools are full of the children of those with good *songbun*.

Due to the effect of socialization over the course of two or three generations, *songbun* has outgrown its political origins. If you possess good *songbun*, you will end up studying and working mainly with others of good *songbun*, in superior schools and workplaces. You will probably live in a relatively decent apartment building, alongside others with good *songbun*. Your relatives will have good jobs, and they will thus be able to pull strings to help you out in case of any trouble. All of this will seem natural to you.

You will likely marry someone of good *songbun*, too. If you happen to fall in love with someone with bad *songbun*, that person will probably be poorer and of lower social value than you, prompting opposition from your parents. In Korean culture, parental opposition is an insurmountable obstacle to a match,[4] in a majority of cases; this is still just about true even in South Korea, where most survey recipients say they would not defy their parents by marrying someone they did not approve of. In any case, most of your peers will be of similar *songbun* status to you, so the actual chance of meeting and falling in love with a person of different *songbun* will be quite low.

Ultimately, *songbun* acts as an anti-meritocratic force, giving unearned advantages and disadvantages to people based on an accident of birth. In that respect, it is little different from the class system found in the UK, or one could argue, the whole concept of inherited wealth in any capitalist society. The

---

4. Interestingly, Kim Kyong Hui and Jang Song Thaek were exceptions to this. Jang came from a relatively "ordinary" background, and Kim Il Sung thus opposed their union. Kim Kyong Hui defied her father, though, and eventually, Kim Il Sung came to grudgingly accept his lower-class son-in-law.

There is also the small matter of Kim Jong Il's own choice of consort, Ko Yong Hui, Kim Jong Un's mother. Ko Yong Hui's father lived in Japan for many years, and even worked at a factory owned by the Japanese Ministry of War. Unlike with Kim Jong Il's mother Kim Jong Suk, attempts to make Ko Yong Hui into any sort of "national mother" figure have failed, not least in part because of her "hostile class" background.

difference is that *songbun* was deliberately designed and implemented by an enthusiastic government, thus ensuring class distinctions entrenched themselves very quickly following the almost total leveling of the social hierarchy caused by the Korean War.[5]

Thankfully, the influence of *songbun* has been somewhat eroded in the post-famine era. Other than fear of punishment, money is the prime motivating force in today's North Korea. If one is successful in business, one cannot buy better *songbun* itself. One can, however, buy the *effects* of better *songbun*—university places, coveted jobs, high-quality apartments, medical care, greater freedom of movement, and immunity from prosecution or harsh punishment, in most cases. This is a phenomenon that has been observed in many countries making the change from a feudal to a market-based system. Many of the growing entrepreneurial class have poor *songbun*, but it scarcely makes a difference in their lives. And if one has plenty of money, one can always marry into a high-status family.

One source talks of a North Korean friend who worked in the government, but had limited prospects due to poor *songbun*. The man in question decided to bribe his superiors instead, and was duly awarded a better position. He used his improved status to collect more bribes for himself, seeing his original bribe essentially as an investment. This practice of bribing to gain better jobs is now very common in North Korea (though there are limits as to how high one can reach). Officialdom is full of lower-level people bribing their higher-ups, in the hope of moving up the hierarchy. Under a "normal" gov-

---

5. One has to qualify this with "almost" in the case of South Korea as often, former Japanese collaborators were able to gain favor from the US military administration and then later, the Syngman Rhee government.

ernment, money is collected by the top levels and distributed downwards; under the post-famine DPRK government, it travels the other way.

One must not fall into the common trap of assuming that *songbun* has been completely circumvented, though. While corruption and capitalism are providing the sharp operator and the talented outlier with opportunities to rise that they would never have had under Kim Il Sung, *songbun* still gives great advantages to some, whilst holding others back. *Songbun* is no longer the sole deciding factor, but it is a gigantic head start.

If one looks at the typical senior North Korean official, one will see a person of high *songbun*, who has a highly-ranked cousin in the military, and a brother with a good position in the State Security Department, for instance.[6] The official in question may not be particularly intelligent, or hard-working; in fact, his virtual inheritance of position (due to good *songbun* and family ties) likely incentivizes him to be lazy. His main activity is the collection of bribes. Meanwhile, the low *songbun* trader who has to bribe him to keep operating her small business is, in meritocratic terms, more deserving due to her hard work. Her standard of living is much better than it was before North Korean society became hopelessly corrupt, but the high *songbun* official collecting payoffs from her is the one who gets to live a truly enviable lifestyle.

Similarly, ambitious and hard-working officials (who also, of course, owe their position to high *songbun*) are the ones who are best placed to take advantage of major business opportunities, such as the construction boom in Pyongyang, or resource extraction. Those barred from such opportunities are

---

6. Again, though, one must note this kind of nepotism is not unique to North Korea.

becoming increasingly disgruntled, according to a number of sources. When defections from North Korea became commonplace in the wake of the famine, the driving force behind the trend was the simple need to eat. Today, though, more and more defectors were actually able to live relatively well in North Korea, but simply feel aggrieved that they have hit a ceiling due to their social status: *baljeon mothaettda* ("I couldn't develop myself [in North Korea]") is now one of the reasons being cited for defection.

A Brief Historical Diversion

During the 1590s, Japan launched a series of invasions against Korea, collectively known as the Imjin Waeran. The early seventeenth century also saw invasions from Manchuria, leading Joseon Dynasty Korea to become a tributary state of the Chinese Qing Dynasty in 1637. Hundreds of thousands perished, and many more were displaced, as a result of these events. Inevitably, social re-ordering also occurred. The ruling *yangban* aristocracy lost some of its power, allowing a new, rising class of merchants to gain a degree of wealth and status, much as is happening today in North Korea. Those in the merchant class took advantage of the changed situation to marry into down-and-out *yangban* families, or bribe their way into *yangban* family record books, thereby cementing their status.

These developments did not mean the end of the Joseon Dynasty, or the *yangban*. The eventual result was the replenishment of the Korean elite with new blood and new ideas. Officials and scholars of the time slowly started to fall under the influence of *silhak* (practical learning), which emphasized improvement through science and technology, and land reform, among other innovations. In such an environment, King Yeongjo (r. 1724–76) went on to lead Korea into a new period of enlightenment and prosperity.

As a cause of both human misery and social re-ordering, the famine of the mid-1990s could be compared to the tumult of the late sixteenth and early seventeenth centuries. Today's *yangban* North Korean—the high-*songbun* government official—is adapting to a new reality in which the most valued official is the one who learns how to do profitable business. Meanwhile, one of the most desirable matches for his son is the daughter of a successful trading family. One class is not replacing the other; much like in the mid–late Joseon era, they are blending as part of the existing social order. Furthermore, today's younger North Korean government official is a pragmatist, open to new ideas—in contrast to his older counterparts.

What does this mean for the future? Of course, external circumstances are different, and social change moves at an incomparably faster pace than it did 300–400 years ago. Nobody would expect the DPRK to last six centuries, as the Joseon Dynasty did. However, the comparison with Joseon Korea does at least mean we should be a little skeptical of claims that social change in North Korea will inevitably bring about the downfall of the regime within the short or medium term. Collapse is just one of several possibilities; what seems more likely is a gradual opening up and reform from within. In terms of minimizing human suffering, this may even be the most desirable outcome.

Pyongyang vs. the Rest

The social composition of Pyongyang shows the desire of the government to pack its capital city with loyalists. Over the years, low *songbun* people have been banished to remote regions, leaving Pyongyang an upper class-heavy place. In 1973, for instance, Kim Jong Il ordered intense *songbun*-based investigations into all Workers' Party members after becoming Director of the OGD. The eventual result after three years of effort was 500,000 banishments. He replaced them with 600,000 new young members in their twenties and thirties, in order to create a new generation of elites specifically loyal to him. This was a nationwide project, but Pyongyang felt its effects disproportionately. It would, however, be an overstatement to claim that Pyongyang has no residents of low *songbun* backgrounds—after all, there is plenty of poverty and even malnutrition in Pyongyang (which would suggest lower *songbun*, other things being equal), and these days, one can bribe one's way in as well—but certainly, the great privilege of living in the capital is one enjoyed predominantly by the "loyal" class.

North Korea has a center-periphery divide that goes far beyond the matter of *songbun*, though. Government focus and spending, including that directed toward attention-grabbing projects like amusement parks, is disproportionately centered on the capital. However, in the eyes of the North Korean public, Pyongyang is special: children are excited to go on school trips there; and the bribe paid to enter Pyongyang is much more expensive than bribes to go anywhere else.

There are important cultural differences, too, that have little to do with politics. Seoulites sometimes call rural South Koreans *chon-nom* ("country bastard," equivalent to "bumpkin"), and similarly, a Pyongyangite visiting the countryside would probably be inclined to look down upon the locals. Country folk would in turn tell you that Pyongyang dwellers are cold, and only make friends with those who prove useful to them—exactly the same criticism rural South Koreans make of Seoul people.

The most "country" place would probably be Kangwon Province, which is divided into two by the DMZ.[7] Kangwon people are generally the most isolated from both the important social changes being led by the northeastern cities like Chongjin, and the public-private capitalism and conspicuous consumption of Pyongyang. They have an informational disadvantage, and as a result have more genuine feelings of loyalty to the state than the citizens of either city. Some defectors have called Kangwon and other country folk[8] *sunjinhae* (pure, naive) in contrast with the *kkaen saramdeul* (literally "people who have woken up" or "the enlightened," i.e., those who know the "reality" of North Korea), who are predominantly found in cities and the northeast. If there were ever an uprising in North Korea, it would be much more likely to start in Chongjin than Kangwon.

---

7. Kangwon people on the South Korean side, too, are sometimes considered innocent, naive country folk, as can be seen in the movie *Welcome to Dongmakgol* (2005).

8. Other than the fact that the old landlord and tenant system is gone, country life in North Korea is actually very similar to how it would have been a hundred years ago. Farmers plow the fields with oxen, and dig by hand. Fertilizer is a rare luxury. And unlike in Pyongyang (or Seoul for that matter), community and family life is still very close-knit.

 Interestingly, there is a possibility we will look back one or two decades from now and identify farmers as having been at the cutting edge of North Korean reform. Under the "6.28 Instructions" first announced in 2012, farmers are now allowed to keep 30 percent of their output for themselves. Yields have reportedly risen strongly; Deng Xiaoping would approve.

While both Pyongyang and the northeast are full of "the enlightened," those in the former have much more to gain from tolerating the contradictions of the DPRK system, since they have privileged status as residents of the capital. Northeasterners, though, are the ones who have been let down the most by the government. When the Public Distribution System started to break down, the two northeastern provinces of North Hamgyong and Ryanggang (along with South Hamgyong) were the first to lose out, having their supplies completely stopped in 1994. Kim Jong Il reportedly harbored a personal hatred for North Hamgyong, considering it rebellious and hostile to his interests. It is no coincidence that North Hamgyong has long been used as a place of exile for political undesirables. It is the furthest province from Pyongyang, and is thus a natural dumping ground for those whom the regime does not trust.

Both provinces have a great deal of contact with China, too. A huge range of goods, including DVDs and USB sticks containing foreign media, and illegal fashions, crosses into the northeast first. It is also no coincidence that a disproportionately high number of defectors come from North Hamgyong and Ryanggang, considering their geographic proximity and the narrowness in places of the Tumen River, the waterway separating the two countries. Settled defectors can, of course, send money and information back to their relatives—further increasing the psychological distance between these relatives remaining in the northeast, and the government in Pyongyang.

In relative terms, North Hamgyong is left to its own devices. This is why women there can dress more fashionably, and why policing there is less strict. As a general rule, North Hamgyong people can live comparatively freely by North Korean standards, as long as they do not do anything that the government considers a threat.

There are two other provinces that border China, Chagang and North Pyongan. They are in the northwest of the country, but are also not so far away from Pyongyang. Border security in those two provinces has generally been tighter, and the financial and psychological investment from the state has also been greater.

Hwagyo

North Korea is often claimed to be the world's most ethnically homogeneous country. Though probably true, this statement obscures the fact that there are actually a small number of ethnic Chinese (*hwagyo*) living in North Korea. Over the years, the North Korean government has made efforts to remove them (though in ways that would not anger ally Beijing), in keeping with the extreme ethnic nationalism that pervades the regime mindset. However, 8,000–10,000 *hwagyo* still remain, divided between Pyongyang and northern cities like Sinuiju and Chongjin. These Chinese passport-holding descendants of nineteenth century immigrants today possess disproportionate influence over North Korean society and trade in comparison to their head count, despite their outsider status.

Before Deng Xiaoping began the process of opening China up, the North Korean standard of living was the envy of the average Chinese. Furthermore, the horrors of the Cultural Revolution of the 1960s meant that *hwagyo* were typically happy to remain in North Korea, a comparatively stable and improving country at the time. Within North Korea, though, *hwagyo* were among the poorest members of society. They were barred from joining the Workers' Party, due to their ethnic origin, and were thus limited in terms of career prospects. Older North Koreans can recall the sight of Chinese beggars on the streets of their cities.

The fortunes of *hwagyo* began a dramatic reversal in the 1980s, when they were given the right to visit China at will, as well as the right to invite Chinese relatives into North Korea. At the time, very few other North Koreans were able to leave the country, meaning that *hwagyo* were effectively handed a monopoly on private trade with a newly-capitalist giant—transforming them into the richest identifiable group of people in North Korea, outside of the elite. They took North Korean mushrooms and seafood to China, and returned with electronic goods and clothing.[9] When the famine hit in the mid-1990s, *hwagyo* started importing food into North Korea as well.

Thus as North Koreans experienced their greatest period of hardship, Chinese North Koreans were enjoying wealth and status—mirroring perfectly the changing fortunes of the two countries. And even in the current era of a market-driven North Korea, *hwagyo* have been able to preserve their advantage. They are richer, and better-connected in China. This gives them a head start over other traders.

Hwagyo are also a reliable source of the kind of products and information that the North Korean government goes to great lengths to stop its citizens from obtaining. As with other traders, they bring in DVDs of South Korean, American, and Chinese movies and drama serials; Chinese cell phones; and, freely tunable radio sets and televisions. In the other direction, *hwagyo* were also the main movers in the illicit export of antiques stolen from graves and archaeological sites in the 1990s. This was a fantastically lucrative business—locals would hand

---

9. For more on this, please see Andrei Lankov's article "Chinese Community in NK" at http://www.koreatimes.co.kr/www/news/opinion/2009/02/166_13968.html

over thousand-year old *koryo cheongja* celadon vases for the equivalent of around US$50, but by the time they reached Seoul via China, they would go for US$5,000 or more. It was also a trade that enraged the authorities; looters and dealers of such artifacts were frequently executed.

Furthermore, as foreign citizens, *hwagyo* are not required to attend propaganda sessions, or even send their children to North Korean schools. They are allowed to possess freely tunable radios, and listen to whatever they please. *Hwagyo* thus have no reason not to be *kkaen saramdeul*, and in being able to freely visit China, they are completely aware of what the DPRK authorities need to do if they want to improve the standard of living of the North Korean people. North Koreans they come into contact with easily become aware of it, too.

In some ways, knowledge of China is even more subversive than knowledge of South Korea. Though most North Koreans already know that South Koreans are much richer than they are, it is still possible for the authorities to label the South an American "puppet," or a place that sold its soul. China, on the other hand, was a brother-in-arms with a similar economic system. The once-impoverished Chinese have experienced great progress by discarding that economic system, and now lead much more prosperous lives than North Koreans. North Koreans find this particularly galling, and increasingly refuse to believe false claims that their impoverishment is a result of natural disasters, or the tough geopolitical situation of their country. Perhaps for this reason, it is now said that the government is stepping up surveillance on *hwagyo*, and cracking down on their business activities.

Will North Korea Collapse?

As we have seen, North Koreans who step out of line face the threat of what is probably the most brutal penal system in the world today. But owing to the complete breakdown of the DPRK's social contract in the wake of the famine, North Koreans are increasingly likely to disregard the government's rules of economic and social behavior. Furthermore, the officials whose job it is to enforce compliance are just as transgressive as ordinary citizens. Usually, a bribe is all it takes to make a problem go away in North Korea.

North Korea's new "system" is unfair and Darwinian, but it at least gives the average person a sense of agency, and the chance to earn a (admittedly meager) living. Furthermore, it is a system that is now so entrenched that the government itself must adapt to it, whether or not it wants to. This has included offering salaries at a nationally-owned steel mill that reflect real market prices; allowing farmers to keep some of what they produce; and, allowing people to pay their way out of state employment—thus freeing them up to conduct their own private business. The regime feels compelled to follow this path, just as they feel compelled to talk up a new era of prosperity and consumerism for North Koreans in their propaganda.

The DPRK government is basically bankrupt. The Public Distribution System is dead to the vast majority of North Koreans. Marketization is the only thing keeping North Korea from suffering a fresh catastrophe, and as such, the government needs to accept it at a minimum level in order to stave off collapse. But now the ball has started rolling, who knows where it will end up?

Having said all this, the authors remain doubtful about the possibility of regime collapse. A good number of DPRK-watchers have been predicting collapse and reunification under the Seoul government for decades, and have come away disappointed. As noted, political control is still intact, and any challenge to it is met with extreme ruthlessness. Furthermore, the new, rising capitalist class generally seeks to *join* the existing elite through marriage and business ties, rather than undermine it. And existing elites themselves have the greatest access to new business opportunities, giving these powerful people a strong vested interest in not seeking to undermine the system.

Even in the wake of the obviously destabilizing execution of Jang Song Thaek, there is little evidence that the regime is on the brink. The succession of Kim Jong Un has gone through, propaganda supporting him is everywhere, and a coalition of powerful people around him has control. Of course, it is hard to say which of two identifiable groups—the OGD and the Kim family, which together form the nexus of DPRK power—has the upper hand, or what the state of relations between the two is. But we can say that no other group possesses the organizational capability to mount a challenge. As depressing as it may sound, the situation is theirs to mess up.

At the same time, the broader geopolitical environment in which North Korea exists is surprisingly well-balanced. Despite the common perception that "crazy" Pyongyang could stage a nuclear attack on South Korea or even the United States, the leadership has absolutely no incentive to consider such a suicidal action. The DPRK leadership may be many things, but irrational is not one of them. Furthermore, the US and South Korea also have obvious disincentives against ever attacking North Korea—the most important being the DPRK's nuclear program and Chinese support for the status quo. Beijing may be dissatisfied with Pyongyang these days, but the continued existence of North Korea remains in the strategic interests of China. Additionally, those who claim sanctions could push the DPRK to breaking point overlook the fact that Pyongyang is awash with luxury goods and enjoying economic growth, despite years of restrictions.

The authors therefore believe that the most likely scenario for North Korea in the short and medium term is the gradual opening of the country under the rule of the current regime. But North Korea, this profit-driven, feudalistic, traditional Korean "socialist paradise," has long had the power to surprise. No-one really knows what the North Korea of 10 or 20 years hence will look like. In the meantime, we continue to watch with a mixture of frustration and hope.

Index